Summary

The World Bank Group supports privatization in the context of its broader goals of economic development and the reduction of poverty.[1] An efficient private sector makes essential contributions to the attainment of these goals. Among the means available for promoting private sector development is the privatization of state-owned enterprises (SOEs). Privatization, when correctly conceived and implemented, fosters efficiency, encourages investment (and thus new growth and employment), and frees public resources for investment in infrastructure and social programs.

Privatization is a complement to, not a replacement for, the other aspects of the development of the private sector in the World Bank's member countries. In many instances privatization will be less important for the growth of the private sector than the emergence of new private businesses. Measures that support free entry by private operators will be crucial in shifting the balance of economic activities from the public to the private domain.

This book reviews the experience of countries with state-owned enterprises and with the privatization of these enterprises. The main lessons of experience are clear:

- Private ownership itself makes a difference. Some state-owned enterprises have been efficient and well managed for some periods, but government ownership seldom permits sustained good performance over more than a few years. The higher probability of efficient performance in private enterprise needs to be considered in choosing whether to invest public funds in SOEs or in health, education, and other social programs.
- The process of privatization, although not simple, can work and has worked; this is true for a variety of enterprises in a variety of settings, including poor countries.

These lessons are already being put into practice. Privatization is widespread and accelerating. More than eighty countries have launched ambitious efforts to privatize their state-owned enterprises. Since 1980, more than 2,000 SOEs have been privatized in developing countries and 6,800 worldwide. Up to 1990, many of the SOEs sold in Bank borrower countries were small or medium in size. The past two years, however, have witnessed an increase not only in the number of large SOEs being sold or readied for sale but also in the number of countries adopting privatization and in the pace of sales.

The World Bank Group has actively supported privatization in more than 180 Bank operations, 50 advisory support and investment operations by the International Finance Corporation (IFC), and three projects by the Multilateral Investment Guarantee Agency (MIGA). Because the three institutions have complementary roles, Bank Group support adds up to more than the sum of its parts.

Why Privatize?

Developing countries have created SOEs for many reasons: to balance or replace weak private sectors, to produce higher investment ratios and extract a capital surplus for investment in the economy, to transfer technology to strategic sectors, to generate employment, and to make goods available at lower cost. Although many SOEs have been productive and profitable, a large number have been economically inefficient, incurred heavy financial losses, and absorbed disproportionate shares of domestic credit.

Of particular concern to governments is the burden that loss-making SOEs place on hard-pressed public budgets. SOE losses as a percentage of gross domestic product (GDP) reached 9 percent in Argentina and Poland in 1989; through the 1980s about half of Tanzania's 350 SOEs persistently ran losses that had to be covered from public funds; in Ghana from 1985 to 1989 the annual outflow from government to fourteen core SOEs averaged 2 percent of GDP; and in China about 30 percent of SOEs were loss-making in 1991. The losses have important consequences: Mexico's minister of finance has noted that a fraction of the $10 billion in losses incurred by the state-owned steel complex would have been enough to bring potable water, sewerage, hospitals, and educational facilities to an entire region of the country (Aspe 1991).[2]

Virtually all developing countries, beginning in the 1970s and continuing through the 1980s, adopted programs to remedy the causes of poor SOE performance—but without changing ownership. The World Bank, through its lending and policy dialogue, actively worked with borrowers to implement these reforms. Many of the reform programs had positive results. But they proved difficult to implement and even harder to sustain, both in industrial countries—such as New Zealand and

Privatization

The Lessons of Experience

Sunita Kikeri
John Nellis
Mary Shirley ·

The World Bank
Washington, D.C.

1992 The International Bank for Reconstruction
d Development / THE WORLD BANK
18 H Street, N.W.
ashington, D.C. 20433

The findings, interpretations, and conclusions expressed in this
study are entirely those of the authors and should not be
attributed in any manner to the World Bank, to its affiliated
organizations, or to members of its Board of Executive Directors
or the countries they represent.

Library of Congress Cataloging-in-Publication Data

Kikeri, Sunita.
    Privatization : the lessons of experience / Sunita Kikeri, John
Nellis, Mary Shirley.
        p.   cm.
    Includes bibliographical references.
    ISBN 0-8213-2181-1
    1. Privatization. 2. Privatization—Europe, Eastern.
3. Privatization—Asia, Central.   I. Nellis, John R.   II. Shirley,
Mary M., 1945–   .   III. Title.
HD3850.K55   1992
338.9—dc20   92-27381
                                                                  CIP

Contents

Acknowledgments   *iv*

Summary   *1*

1. Objectives and Scope   *13*

2. Why Privatize? History and Evidence   *15*
   Past Reform Efforts   *16*
   The Turn toward Privatization   *20*
   The Privatization Record to Date   *22*
   The Impact of Privatization   *24*
   Support for Privatization by the World Bank Group   *32*

3. Objectives and Strategy for Privatization   *39*
   Conditions for Success   *39*
   Defining Objectives   *43*
   What, How Much, and How Fast to Sell   *48*
   Privatizing Management   *49*
   Full versus Partial Sale   *52*

4. Implementation   *54*
   Preparing for Sale   *54*
   Pricing and Valuation   *62*
   Financing   *64*
   Managing Privatization   *70*

5. Privatization in Eastern Europe and Central Asia   *73*
   Past Performance   *73*
   The Turn toward Privatization   *73*
   Obstacles to Privatization and Ways around Them   *75*
   Mass Privatization   *77*

Notes   *79*

Bibliography   *83*

Acknowledgments

This study was carried out under the direction of Nancy Birdsall and Lawrence H. Summers. Stuart Bell and Charlie Thomas provided outstanding research assistance. Nissim Ezekiel, Koichiro Fukui, Ahmed Galal, Pierre Guislain, Woonki Sung, Yoshiro Takano, Dileep Wagle, and Gerald West made valuable contributions. Many other World Bank Group staff offered useful comments and ideas. Excellent secretarial assistance was provided by Gloria Orraca-Tetteh.

Japan—and in developing countries. In the Republic of Korea, where a reform program put a group of SOEs in the black for three years in the mid-1980s, losses have since reoccurred. A number of SOEs that the Bank's *World Development Report 1983* cited as well on the road to improved performance because of exemplary reform efforts—manufacturing SOEs in Pakistan, the Senegalese bus company, and fertilizer SOEs in Turkey—either have failed to improve in performance or have deteriorated. Growing recognition by governments of the limited and unsustainable nature of past reforms helped fuel the drive toward privatization in the 1980s.

SOEs can be placed on an economic-financial performance spectrum that ranges from very good to very bad. Although the same is true for private firms, there is considerable evidence indicating that the median point on the private enterprise spectrum lies higher than the median on the public enterprise spectrum. This is true under all market and country conditions. The decision concerning what to privatize and what to reform should thus tend toward privatization as the outcome most likely to produce positive gains. The likelihood that SOEs will cause problems places the burden of proof squarely on their advocates. The evidence in this book repeatedly points to the conclusion that ownership itself matters.

The Impact of Privatization

The benefits from properly executed privatization have proved to be considerable, as is shown by cases in Latin America, Africa, and Asia, as well as in industrial countries. Privatization improved domestic welfare in eleven of twelve cases analyzed by the World Bank in Chile, Malaysia, Mexico, and the United Kingdom.[3] Productivity went up in nine of the twelve and showed no decline in the other three. Expanded investment and diversification of production resulted in rapid growth in many of the firms studied; for example, the Chilean telephone company doubled its capacity in the four years following sale. Labor as a whole was not worse off, even taking into account all layoffs and forced retirements. Consumers were better off or were unaffected by sale in a majority of cases. Buyers of the firms made money, but in the main the other stakeholders—labor, consumers, and government—gained as well.

Studies and data from outside the World Bank also show that privatized companies grow more rapidly and are better able to contain their costs than before privatization. In forty-one firms fully or partially privatized by public offerings in fifteen countries (most of them industrial, but the list includes Chile, Jamaica, and Mexico) returns on sales, assets, and equity increased and internal efficiency improved because of better utilization of physical and human resources. The firms improved their capital structure and increased capital expenditures. Their work forces also rose slightly, thanks to higher investments.

Most privatization success stories come from high- or middle-income countries. It is harder to privatize in low-income settings, where the process is more difficult to launch. But even in low-income countries the results of some privatizations have been highly positive, as shown below.

Revenues from sales have been large in some countries, but in most, net revenues have been modest because of small transaction size, the costs of settling enterprise debts, and payment of delinquent taxes and transaction fees and because many sales have been on credit. More important, privatization has reduced subsidies to SOEs and has led to increases in government income when taxes paid by privatized firms have exceeded the sums previously paid by SOEs. In Mexico transfers and subsidies from the government to SOEs declined by 50 percent between 1982 and 1988; the stabilization program after the 1982 shock was the most important cause, but privatizations, which began in 1984, helped lock in these reductions.

Conditions for Success

Two main factors affect the outcomes—in terms of economic productivity and consumer welfare—of privatization (see figure 1). One is the nature of the market into which the enterprise will be divested—that is, whether it is competitive or noncompetitive. Privatization of enterprises in competitive and, in particular, tradable sectors such as industry, airlines, agriculture, and retail operations is likely to yield solid and rapid economic benefits as long as there are not economywide distortions that hinder competition. Even with such distortions, privatization can have the benefit of reducing the fiscal burden of SOE subsidies and exposing fully the costs of the distortions.

The second factor is country conditions: the overall macroeconomic policy framework and capacity to regulate. Privatization of both competitive and noncompetitive enterprises will yield more immediate and greater benefits the more market-friendly the policy environment (the top panels of the figure). For this reason, the World Bank Group often supports privatization as one part of an overall government program of exchange rate, fiscal, trade, and price reforms. When privatization involves enterprises in noncompetitive markets—usually large SOEs operating as natural monopolies in such areas as power, water supply, and

Figure 1. Privatization: A Framework for Decisionmaking

Country conditions	Enterprise conditions	
	Competitive	Noncompetitive
High capacity to regulate; market-friendly	*Decision* • Sell	*Decision* • Ensure or install appropriate regulatory environment • Then consider sale
Low capacity to regulate; market-unfriendly	*Decision* • Sell, with attention to competitive conditions	*Decision* • Consider privatization of management arrangements • Install market-friendly policy framework • Install appropriate regulatory environment • Then consider sale

telecommunications—a legal and regulatory system must be in place to protect consumers. Good policies and regulatory capacity are correlated with income; thus, middle-income countries tend to be in a better position to privatize rapidly enterprises in noncompetitive sectors.

The privatization process itself is also easier if the enterprise is in a competitive sector and the environment is market-friendly. The sale of an enterprise in a competitive sector in a favorable country setting (the upper left-hand panel in the figure) requires little more than adequate attention to transparency in the transaction and the lifting of any inappropriate regulations or price controls. In unfavorable country settings, where the existing private sector is small, capital markets are thin, and the interest of external investors is limited, the sale of enterprises even in competitive sectors may be more difficult. But the benefits in economic gains are potentially large, especially in comparison with the continued operation of a loss-making SOE.

Privatization turned a near-moribund textile company in Niger into a profitable exporter. A finance corporation in Swaziland, closed as an SOE, became a profitable private company in two years. Privatization helped put an agroindustrial enterprise in Mozambique on a profitable footing. Privatizations succeeded because they brought in owners with the necessary resources and skills and, more important, a direct stake in the performance of the company. They ended enterprises' ready access to government subsidies and protection and often contributed to increased competition. This is not to say that privatization always and only produces positive results; negative outcomes have occurred. It is the task of governments and the agencies assisting them—including the World Bank Group—to structure the enabling environment and the transactions in such a way that the potential of privatization is fulfilled.

For the sale of enterprises in noncompetitive sectors (the right-hand side of the figure), the steps are more numerous and the process is more difficult. The enterprises are larger, foreign investment issues are even more salient, and again—especially in lower-income countries—capital markets are thin. Successful privatization of natural monopolies requires a regulatory framework that separates out potentially competitive activities, establishes the tariff regime, clarifies service goals, develops cost-minimization targets, and creates or strengthens an agency to supervise the process. Governments will need to be alert to ensure free entry whenever competition is possible. Particularly in lower-income countries, contracts, leases, and other ways of privatizing management are a step in the right direction: they are beneficial in their own right, and they launch a transition to full privatization. Even if management of the entire enterprise is not privatized, services such as billing, construction, and office maintenance can be contracted to the private sector.

Implementation

Governments need not attempt to plan the privatization process down to the last detail, but they must set the principles, choose between potentially conflicting objectives, and supervise the fairness and outcome of the process.

Defining the Objectives

The economic benefits of privatization are maximized when governments make improved efficiency the number one goal—by using privatization to enhance competition and by ensuring a competitive market that reinforces the benefits of privatization. Maximization of revenue should not be the primary consideration. It is better to eliminate monopoly power and to unleash potentially competitive activities than to maximize revenues from sales into protected markets. And it is better to construct appropriate regulatory frameworks to protect consumer welfare than to increase revenue by selling into an unregulated market.

Similarly, short-run distributional considerations, although they cannot be ignored, should not be pursued at the cost of managerial competence. Privatization should aim to improve corporate governance, and

that may mean forgoing widely dispersed ownership in fa
owner with enough of a stake to have strong motivation and the c
needed for turning around a troubled SOE. In addition, sale of SO
through public offerings, which is attractive because it mutes the charge
that domestic elites or foreign investors are being favored, is difficult to
launch and manage, and delays have been a common result.

What, How Much, and How Fast to Sell

Many countries began divestiture by selling small and medium-size SOEs
in competitive sectors. Such sales are simple and quick, involve little
restructuring or postsale regulation, and are politically low-risk. Start
small, learn by doing, and move on to larger, more complicated transactions: this was the primary lesson of the successful experience in Mexico.

But there is no single strategy, and the choice of where to begin
depends on investor interest, on government capacity, and on identification of the sectors and enterprises most in need of new investments
and improvements in efficiency. A growing number of governments are
opting to launch their privatization programs with sales of large and
often poorly performing public utilities. They believe that the window
of political opportunity may be but briefly open, that divestiture of a
major SOE will signal commitment to investors and markets, and that the
economic returns of enhanced efficiency in a large firm will outweigh
the potential risks. This strategy has most often been used in Latin
America (for example in Argentina), and to good effect.

Surprisingly, a number of loss-makers have been successfully sold.
Most of the IFC's privatization transactions involved SOEs that were
making recurrent losses; many had actually been closed. These companies required investments for modernization, and privatization provided access to private investment capital.

Privatizing Management

Management contracts, leases, or concessions, as methods of privatizing
management, are particularly beneficial in low-income countries with
weak capital markets and banking institutions, limited investor interest,
and weak regulatory capacity. When management contracts (whereby
the government pays a fee to a private company to manage the firm in
question) are correctly drawn up, the gains can be considerable, but they
necessitate good drafting and good supervisory capacity in government.
Leases provide greater incentives to reduce costs and maintain the
long-term value of the assets, since the private party assumes commer-

.nce-based fee to the government. Conces-
der, in return for a long-term lease, assumes
)enditures and investments. Experience with
ing countries is still both slight and relatively

organizational, and managerial changes, financial
workou..,   shedding—is often a necessary prelude to sale,
especially for la.ᵦ   .irms. (Small and medium-size SOEs can be successfully divested with hardly any prior restructuring.) Changing management and settling the liabilities of the SOE are standard measures in
successful transactions.

Layoffs do not always accompany privatization; in Mexico, Philippines, and Tunisia privatizations actually led to increased employment.
But where large-scale labor shedding is required, it is best handled by
the state. Buyers may demand protection and subsidies in exchange for
taking on excess labor, reducing the efficiency gains from privatization.
The government is better able to mediate union demands and to design
measures for alleviating the social costs through retraining, severance
pay, unemployment insurance, and other elements of the social safety
net. The support of workers has been elicited by undertaking public
awareness campaigns explaining the costs and benefits of privatization
and of the alternatives, by allotting workers free or subsidized shares in
the privatized firms, and by granting adequate severance packages.

Large new investments for plant modernization or rehabilitation prior
to sale should be avoided. Getting the private sector to finance investments and take the risk is a prime reason for privatization in the first
place. There is also little evidence that governments recover the costs of
physical restructuring in the form of higher sales prices.

Pricing and Valuation

Letting the market decide the sale price through competitive bidding is
the optimal method. Enterprise valuation is difficult in the best of
circumstances and is doubly so in developing countries and in former
socialist economies that are undergoing macroeconomic changes. In
these situations, information is weak, comparables are few, and the
market is thin. Although some external or independent valuation is
useful for setting a floor price and ensuring a fair process (particularly
in countries with weak capital markets), technical methods seldom

determine the market price for an enterprise. Overvaluation and unrealistic price expectations can delay the process or even lead to valuations that bear little resemblance to what any buyer will offer.

Financing

Government decisions often compound the financing constraints imposed by weak financial systems. A surprising number of governments have put SOEs on the market while at the same time issuing high-yield, low-risk, tax-free government bonds, which compete with the SOEs as an investment. Some governments have further narrowed the sales market by excluding or favoring certain ethnic groups and by placing restrictions on foreign participation. Ways of satisfying political concerns without curtailing the market include reserving free or subsidized shares for groups that would otherwise not be able to participate, keeping a "golden share" for government (with voting rights restricted to decisions on major changes in the firms), and combining sale of a controlling interest to a foreign investor with widespread distribution of the remaining shares to citizens and employees.

Selling for cash is preferable to accepting debt, even if this means a lower price. Outright sale cleanly severs the link between enterprise and state, and cash sales provide the liquidity needed to pay enterprise liabilities, including severance pay. Many countries have resorted to government-financed sales for debt because financial systems are not deep enough, the SOEs are not sufficiently attractive, and the preferred buyers are illiquid. Lowering the price, selling in tranches, or even giving small assets away may be preferable to lavish use of debt.

Debt-equity swaps can ease financing constraints and help improve a country's investment climate. In Argentina, Chile, and the Philippines, swaps have helped bring foreign investors and commercial banks into transactions that might not have occurred in their absence. Nevertheless, swaps must be used carefully. The government may be better off to sell the asset and use the proceeds to buy back debt on the market. Heavily indebted countries may not have a choice, however, as a large debt overhang may deter investors from buying SOEs—particularly large companies that require new investment. In these circumstances, debt-equity swaps can be useful.

Investors' concerns about whether they can raise sufficient capital to modernize and expand may be a stumbling block to the sale of large SOEs. This is particularly so in infrastructure, where sales income is in local currency, raising worries about convertibility and exchange risks. Recent Latin American experience shows that when macroeconomic and regulatory frameworks are sound, investment capital can usually be raised without any guarantees. But in other cases, where perceptions of country risk are high, some assistance from international agencies and bilateral donors in accessing financial markets may be required to finance investments in newly privatized enterprises. Such support is currently provided to private investors by the IFC and, more recently, through MIGA, which insures noncommercial investment risk.

Managing the Transaction

An important lesson of experience is that transparency is always essential. This means competitive bidding procedures, clear criteria for evaluating bids, disclosure of purchase price and buyer, well-defined institutional responsibilities, and adequate monitoring of the program. Lack of transparency can lead to a perception, justified or not, of unfair dealing and to a popular outcry that can threaten not only privatization but also reform in general. Both transparency and speed are served when policy responsibilities for privatization are centralized in a strong agency, answering to the political top, with a clear mandate and authority and a small, highly competent staff.

Privatization in Eastern Europe and Central Asia

In the former socialist economies, enterprise numbers are larger and the economic and social importance of SOE sectors far greater than in the rest of the world. Whereas in mixed economies privatization is a tool for increasing efficiency, in the former socialist economies many view divestiture as an end in itself, essential to the transformation from a command to a market system.

To date, the number of enterprises divested in former socialist economies (excluding the former German Democratic Republic) is small in relation both to sector size and to early expectations of how fast transfers would take place. The causes of delay include weak legal frameworks; an insufficient (or very expensive imported) auditing, consulting, and financial apparatus; thin local capital markets and lack of liquidity in the population; and suspicion of investors—foreigners because they are foreign, and domestic because they were, usually, part of the *nomenklatura* (the roster of officials approved by the Communist party). It must be recognized that the costs of inaction and delay are very great. Presently, enterprises receive neither central commands nor adequate market signals; this is the worst possible situation. There is a strong case for massive and rapid privatization to create quickly a property-owning

---

Box 1. A Checklist for Privatization

✓ The more market-friendly a country's policy framework—and appropriate policy is correlated with capacity to regulate—the less difficulty it will have in privatizing an SOE, and the higher the likelihood that the sale will turn out positively.

✓ SOEs functioning in competitive markets, or in markets easily made competitive, are prime candidates for privatization. Their sale is simple, compared with that of public monopolies, and they require little or no regulation.

✓ An appropriate regulatory framework must be in place before monopolies are privatized. Failure to regulate properly can hurt consumers and reduce public support for privatization.

✓ Countries can benefit from privatizing management through management contracts, leases, contracting out, or concessions.

✓ The primary objective of privatization should be to increase efficiency—not to maximize revenue (for example, by selling into protected markets) or even to distribute ownership widely at the expense of managerial efficiency.

✓ Rather than restrict the market by excluding foreign investors and favoring certain ethnic groups, governments should experiment with "golden shares" and partial share offerings to win acceptance for foreign and other buyers.

✓ Avoid large new investments in privatization candidates: the risks usually outweigh the rewards. Rather, prepare for sale by carrying out legal, managerial, and organizational changes, financial workouts, and labor shedding.

✓ Experience shows that labor does not, and need not, lose in privatization if governments pay attention to easing the social cost of unemployment through adequate severance pay, unemployment benefits, retraining, and job search assistance.

✓ Ideally, let the market set the price and sell for cash. Realistically, negotiated settlements and financing arrangements or debt-equity swaps may be unavoidable.

✓ In all privatizations, in all countries, the transaction must be transparent.

---

group of sufficient size and political weight that will respond to price signals and support the steps necessary for the transformation.

Innovative methods of privatization are being devised, including giveaway schemes to the population at large (often called "mass privatization"), state-assisted financing, distribution of free or low-cost shares to employees in privatized firms, and use of new types of investment-management companies to run groups of companies and diversify risk. Mistakes are bound to occur, and the emphasis should not be on avoiding risk but on ensuring flexibility. Experimentation with all available privatization methods should be supported. As experience accumulates, the methods that work best should be strengthened, and mistakes or oversights corrected.

Therefore, although the set of tactics optimal for the former socialist economies may not yet be clear, the general strategy for achieving these countries' objectives, given their circumstances, is apparent: privatize; privatize in all possible ways that encourage competition; and adopt methods that do far more than privatize firms one-by-one, including the transformation of all enterprises into joint stock companies.

The lesson that ownership matters has been heeded: increasingly, governments worldwide are moving to tap private management and finance and to privatize. Governments intent on privatizing face a challenge: the benefits of efficiency and innovation only materialize if privatization is done right. The lessons of experience provide guidance on how to privatize successfully (see box 1). The task of the World Bank Group is to assist countries to realize the promise of privatization while minimizing the costs.

1. Objectives and Scope

Governments around the world are privatizing state-owned enterprises in an effort to improve their efficiency and lessen the financial burden they often represent for taxpayers. Although there are exceptions to the rule, the performance of SOEs has been generally disappointing, and the results of previous partial efforts to reform them have been minimal or unenduring. Many governments today seek to privatize virtually all their SOEs, including public utilities and enterprises that were formerly classed as "strategic" (for example, airlines, ports, railways, petrochemicals, and steel and cement manufacturing).

The World Bank Group supports privatization in the context of its broader goals of economic development and poverty reduction. An efficient private sector makes essential contributions to the attainment of these goals, and privatization is one of the means available for promoting private sector development. Privatization, when correctly conceived and implemented, fosters efficiency, encourages investment and thus new growth and employment, and frees public resources for infrastructure and social programs.

Privatization is a complement to, not a replacement for, the other aspects of the development of the private sector in member countries of the World Bank. In many instances privatization will be less important for the growth of the private sector than the emergence of new private businesses. The experience of the Republic of Korea shows that it is possible to restrain the expansion of public enterprises and at the same time encourage the rapid growth and eventual dominance of a dynamic private sector. In quite different circumstances, Hungarian authorities, as well, are pinning their hopes for economic growth more on the many new entrants in the private sector than on privatization. Free entry by private operators is a crucial means of shifting the balance of economic activities from the public to the private domain. The World Bank Group therefore supports approaches to development that rely only in part on privatization where these approaches are based on strong efforts to encourage and sustain competition.

This book reviews experiences with state-owned enterprises and their privatization in developing and industrial countries and extracts salient themes and lessons for the successful design and implementation of such reform. It deals with the privatization of industrial, commercial, manufacturing, and service-producing state-owned enterprises operating in both competitive and noncompetitive markets. It touches only tangentially on privatization of banks and other financial institutions, which raises many additional and different issues—particularly regulation.

Privatization can be defined as the transfer of ownership of SOEs to the private sector by the sale—full or partial—of ongoing concerns or by the sale of assets following liquidation. Sale of the business or of its assets has been the most widely employed and debated form of privatization, and this is the option that is analyzed in greatest detail. Methods of privatizing management but not ownership—through management contracts, leases, and concessions—are examined as alternatives to outright sale.[4]

Recent trends (chapter 2) show that close to 7,000 enterprises have been privatized worldwide since the early 1980s. More than half of these privatizations have taken place in one country–the former German Democratic Republic—but elsewhere too the number of divestitures has been increasing rapidly. Up to 1990s, many of the SOEs sold in developing countries were small or medium in size, but the past few years have witnessed an increase in both the number of large SOEs being sold and the overall pace of privatizations.

Experience from countries such as Argentina, Chile, Guinea, Jamaica, Mexico, and the Philippines (as well as France, New Zealand, and the United Kingdom) demonstrates that private ownership itself makes a difference. Privatization has helped to improve enterprise performance, reduce the fiscal burden and country debt, and improve consumer welfare—when sales are properly structured and implemented and when the market or regulatory environment ensures competitive behavior. Experience also shows that the process of privatization, although not simple, can work and has worked; this is true for a variety of enterprises in a variety of settings, including low-income countries.

Clarity of objectives and strategy are essential for the success of privatization (chapter 3). This involves identifying and resolving policy tradeoffs; establishing the appropriate scope, pace, and sequencing of privatization; and choosing the right methods. Implementation (chapter 4) involves decisions on the restructuring of SOEs prior to sale, the pricing of assets and shares, the financing of sales, and the institutional setup for managing privatization. Privatization issues differ somewhat in Eastern Europe and Central Asia (chapter 5).

2. Why Privatize? History and Evidence

Over the past several decades, developing countries have created SOEs to balance or replace a weak or ideologically unacceptable private sector, to produce higher investment ratios and yield a capital surplus for investment in the economy, to stimulate weak indigenous private sectors, and to transfer technology to "strategic" firms in mining, telecommunications, transport, and heavy industry. By the early 1980s SOEs accounted, on average, for 17 percent of GDP in Sub-Saharan Africa (in a thirteen-country sample for which data were available; see Nellis 1986), for 12 percent in Latin America, for a modest 3 percent in Asia (excluding China, India, and Myanmar), and for 10 percent in mixed economies worldwide. In Eastern Europe and Central Asia SOEs uniformly account for the bulk—as high as 90 percent—of all productive activities.

There are exceptional SOE performers, but evidence from a wide range of countries shows that far too many SOEs have been economically inefficient and have incurred heavy financial losses. Between 1989 and 1991 SOE losses as a percentage of GDP reached 9 percent in Argentina, 8 percent in Yugoslavia, and more than 5 percent, on average, in some Sub-Saharan African countries. In the 1980s about half of Tanzania's more than 350 SOEs ran losses, and in at least one year the losses were so large as to put the entire sector in deficit. In 1991 about 30 percent of all SOEs in China were loss-makers. In Turkey the operating surplus of the sector has been deteriorating since 1985, and the marginal efficiency of SOE capital is half that of the private sector.

In many countries SOEs have become an unsustainable burden on the budget and the banking system, absorbing scarce public resources. Government transfers and subsidies to SOEs amounted to more than 3 percent of GDP in Mexico in 1982, 4 percent of gross national product (GNP) in Turkey in 1990, and 9 percent of GDP in Poland in 1989. In Ghana in the last half of the 1980s the annual average outflow from government to fourteen core SOEs constantly exceeded the meager flows—in the form of dividends and taxes—from the firms to the state.[5]

Despite concerted efforts, the overall performance of SOEs in utilities and infrastructure has often been disappointing. A recent Bank review of the power sector notes that the performance and viability of many SOEs have deteriorated steadily since the 1970s (see World Bank 1991b). Other infrastructure sector reviews reach similar conclusions, pointing out that the problems are particularly acute in lower-income countries. (For telecommunications see Wellenius, Stern, Nulty, and Stern 1989; Ambrose, Hennemeyer, and Chapon 1990.)

Overextended and poorly performing SOEs, when protected by government subsidies, have probably slowed development of the private sector in borrower countries. Government regulations have sometimes acted to block the entry of private firms where they would compete with SOEs. Directed government credit to capital-intensive SOEs has crowded out private firms from credit markets; in Guinea SOEs—which contributed only 25 percent of GDP—absorbed 90 percent of formal domestic bank credit. Inefficient provision of critical inputs by badly managed SOEs has increased the costs of business to those private firms that do exist and has limited the potential for expansion, particularly in smaller firms (World Bank 1991a).

The reasons for poor SOE performance are many. In principle, a state-owned firm should be able to operate as efficiently as a private firm if both function in a competitive setting according to the same rules and incentives. But experience shows that governments find it difficult to level the playing field or to keep it level. Governments have intervened to provide publicly financed support for their public enterprises, discriminated against their private competitors, or both. For example, governments have awarded SOEs monopoly status in competitive or potentially competitive markets; provided them with subsidies, cheap loans and loan guarantees, and tax and duty exemptions; and failed to penalize them for unpaid taxes and utility bills. They have favored SOEs in their bidding for contracts and have allowed them to run up large accounts with public and private suppliers. At the same time, SOEs have often been burdened with noncommercial objectives such as employment creation and regional development, making further subsidies necessary. Despite the protection and subsidies, many SOEs continue to lose money, leading governments—reluctant to face the disruption of bankruptcy—to respond by further limiting or preventing competition.

Past Reform Efforts

During the past twenty years virtually all developing countries have adopted reform programs—short of ownership transfer—to remedy the causes of poor SOE performance. These reforms aimed at (a) exposing SOEs to domestic and external competition and ending preferential treatment in order to create a level playing field; (b) eliminating easy SOE access to credit from the budget and banking system and instituting a hard budget constraint; (c) increasing the autonomy of SOEs and freeing managers from government interference in day-to-day operational decisionmaking and from noncommercial goals; and (d) developing institutional mechanisms, such as contract plans and performance evaluation systems, to hold managers accountable for results.

Recent assessments of SOE reforms reveal that some improvements in performance have indeed taken place (Galal 1991; Shirley and Nellis 1991). But three problems have emerged.

- First, SOE reforms are technically and politically difficult to implement. Often, well-designed programs—granting autonomy to management on decisions to hire, fire, price, and relocate; restructuring boards of directors to diminish the role of sector ministries and civil servants; costing out noncommercial objectives and compensating the enterprise for their fulfillment; keeping commitments on pricing and investment—fall short in implementation.
- Second, performance does improve when the full package is put in place, but the necessary reforms are numerous and hard to coordinate, and the entire reform program has seldom been enacted. For instance, achievement of financial discipline through a hard budget constraint has been difficult without corresponding restrictions on SOE borrowing from the banking sector. Similarly, without increased managerial autonomy and accountability, pay and employment reforms have yielded few results.
- Third, and most important, performance improvements have proved difficult to sustain once the crisis that instigated the reforms has dissipated.

Examples of the difficulty of sustaining SOE reforms come from industrial countries (boxes 2 and 3) and from developing countries at different levels of income and with different initial conditions. In Senegal, for example, despite persistent sectorwide SOE reforms dating back to 1977, overall performance has remained poor. Some improvements took place in the early 1980s, but total SOE losses have continued to climb. Moreover, although Senegalese SOEs with performance contracts performed better than those without such mechanisms, the device failed to impose crucially needed financial discipline. Similar evidence can be cited for many other developing countries.[6] A number of the SOEs that were judged in *World Development Report 1983* to be well on the road to major and

---

Box 2. Ownership Matters: The Case of New Zealand

By the 1980s, the poor financial performance of New Zealand's state-owned trading activities had created an intolerable drain on state resources. To arrest the decline, the government began "corporatizing" its SOEs in 1987 by adopting reforms that made these companies legal entities with clear objectives, operational autonomy, and accountability. This initiative was followed by the privatization of several SOEs, including telecommunications, airlines, and petroleum.

The experience of New Zealand Post and the Electricity Corporation illustrates the clear short-term gains and the potential long-term problems of corporatization. Prior to the reforms, the postal service had consistently operated in the red, and the government had used the New Zealand Post Office, state provider of telecommunications, postal, and banking services, as an employment agency in recessionary periods. In the first year after corporatization, New Zealand Post generated an after-tax profit of $72.1 million, and it has operated profitably ever since. By a wide range of other indicators, the company has registered excellent results (for example, a 15 percent improvement in on-time delivery of high-priority mail between 1987 and 1990). Similarly, in just one year the Electricity Corporation cut the real cost of electricity production by 11 percent and increased power generation per employee by 19 percent.

Nevertheless, in both instances there is concern that pressure for renewed government intervention is growing. The government has not allowed the Electricity Corporation to diversify into areas that private electricity suppliers normally exploit. While this is consistent with SOE regulations, substantial efficiency gains are being sacrificed by the limitation. Pressures to reimpose nationality requirements on the recruitment of top managers are emerging. And in spite of performance improvements, rates of return on capital at the SOEs remain below those in the private sector.

---

enduring performance improvements thanks to exemplary government reform efforts—for example, the Senegalese bus company, fertilizer SOEs in Turkey, and manufacturing SOEs in Pakistan—either have not improved in performance or have deteriorated.

In many Asian countries, too, SOE reforms have not been sustained. For three years after the introduction of a performance evaluation system and other reforms in Korea in 1986, no SOE in the system recorded a loss.[7] But the government proved unable to resist wage demands by workers, and in 1990 SOE losses reoccurred and totaled 26,570 million won, making that year the second-worst on record. Between 1981 and

Box 3. Japanese Railways: Reforms on the Road to Privatization

Between 1964 and 1986 Japanese National Railways (JNR)—Japan's largest SOE—recorded staggering losses. A recent World Bank study in cooperation with the Japan Economic Research Institute (Fukui 1992) shows that despite five separate attempts at full-scale reform, performance continuously deteriorated. The JNR's annual losses exceeded $7 billion in the mid-1970s and $10 billion in the mid-1980s. Over this period the company received subsidies of more than $57 billion and ran its long-term debt up to $286 billion, or 11 percent of GNP. Past reforms had foundered, largely because management and labor had few incentives to cut costs, raise productivity, and maximize profits. For example, 200,000 surplus employees remained on the payroll, and the JNR could not respond flexibly to rapid growth in competing modes of transport. Furthermore, past reforms did not insulate the JNR against political interference, and the company continued to invest in unprofitable, remote routes.

In 1981, with strong support from the prime minister, the Provisional Committee on Administrative Reform was formed to explore further reform options. Its report, issued in 1982, called for the breakup and eventual sale of the JNR and the establishment of a high-level supervisory committee to devise the specifics of the JNR's privatization strategy. The committee, set up the following year, skillfully leveraged public opinion, which had already turned against the JNR as a result of frequent labor strikes, to ensure that the privatization process stayed on track. In 1987 the JNR was reorganized into seven smaller joint stock companies—six regional passenger lines and one nationwide freight line—and a profit-centered corporate culture was introduced. Deep cuts were made in the labor force, from 358,000 in fiscal 1983 to 191,000 in fiscal 1990—a 47 percent reduction. Long-term debt in the amount of $197 billion, along with real estate, was reassigned to the JNR Settlement Corporation. Legal restrictions that prevented the JNR from diversifying into other businesses were lifted, and Diet approval for the new joint stock companies' budgets was no longer required.

The changes produced significant performance gains, even after allowing for the removal of debt from the joint stock companies' balance sheets and for the effects of economic growth. Between 1986 and 1990, for example, the volume of passenger transport increased at an average annual rate of 5 percent; operating costs for passenger rail fell by 11 percent; revenues per employee rose from $118,000 to $175,000; the joint stock companies as a group moved from an annual operating loss of $4.3 billion to a profit of $3.6 billion; and subsidies were sharply reduced. And whereas the JNR had raised its fares in every year but one after 1981, the

(Box continues on the following page.)

Box 3 (continued)

joint stock companies have not raised their passenger and freight rates since they began operating in fiscal 1987. (The 3 percent fare increase in 1989 was due to the introduction of a consumption tax on all goods and services.) Moreover, the quality of service has improved.

In the JNR case, corporatization and deregulation clearly unleashed competitive pressures that helped improve the efficiency and quality of service. The government made the sale of shares the goal of the program to ensure that the reforms would have bite. Public offerings of three of the joint stock companies are being mapped out for the last quarter of fiscal 1992.

1988 Bangladesh carried out a reform program for industrial SOEs that included increased managerial autonomy, financial restructuring, and employment and wage changes. Despite these reforms, SOE performance deteriorated throughout the 1980s. Their average operating deficit grew, and net transfers from the state to SOEs increased from 0.8 percent of GDP in 1986 to 3.2 percent of GDP in 1989.

In China a restructuring program was launched in the 1980s to stem SOEs' losses and improve their efficiency by strengthening bankruptcy legislation and introducing competition from private enterprise. The reforms led to rapid growth of the private sector (the share of SOEs in industrial production dropped from close to 70 percent in 1986 to 53 percent in 1990), and the introduction of a "responsibility system" brought about improved performance in at least some state-owned industrial firms. Total factor productivity in state enterprises rose at a respectable 3 percent a year between 1984 and 1988, although this was well below the 6 percent rate of collective enterprises. (Figure 2 reveals a correlation, at the province level, between a higher share of privately produced industrial output and higher total factor productivity.) Close to 30 percent of all SOEs, however, still incur losses that absorb a sixth of the government's budgetary expenditures.

The Turn toward Privatization

Both SOEs and private firms can be placed on an economic-financial performance spectrum that ranges from very good to very bad. Considerable evidence indicates, however, that the median point on the private enterprise spectrum lies higher than the median point on the public enterprise spectrum. This is true under all market and country condi-

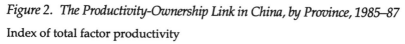

Figure 2. The Productivity-Ownership Link in China, by Province, 1985–87

Index of total factor productivity

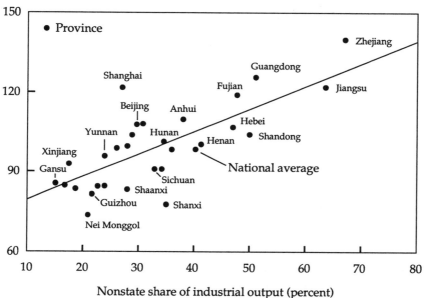

Nonstate share of industrial output (percent)

Note: Because of space limitations, only selected provinces are identified.
Source: Xiao 1991. By permission of JAI Press, Inc., Greenwich, Conn.

tions. The decision concerning what to privatize and what to reform thus tends toward privatization as the outcome most likely to produce positive gains. At the very least, the burden of proof is on those who espouse the creation or maintenance of SOEs. The evidence in this book repeatedly points to the conclusion that ownership itself matters.

Disappointed with the high costs and poor performance of SOEs, and faced with the modest and unenduring nature of reforms that do not involve change in ownership, many governments have turned to privatization. They hope that new private owners will increase the efficiency with which the firms use resources and will decrease the financial demands made by SOEs on strained government budgets.

Governments have also privatized to increase the size and dynamism of the private sector; to distribute ownership more widely in the population at large; to encourage and facilitate private sector investment, from both domestic and foreign sources, for modernization and rehabilitation; to generate revenues for the state; to reduce the administrative burden on the state; and—in the case of the former socialist countries—to launch and sustain the transformation of the economy from a command to a market model.

The Privatization Record to Date

Privatization is widespread and growing (figure 3). Approximately 70 percent of the 6,800-plus sales have taken place in industrial countries— 66 percent of them over the past eighteen months in the former German Democratic Republic alone. Among developing countries (figure 4), former socialist economies in Eastern Europe account for more than 800 sales or liquidations of state-owned firms.[8] Latin America accounts for close to 40 percent of developing country sales, with Chile and Mexico making up the bulk of the activity. Sub-Saharan Africa accounts for 17

Figure 3. Number of SOEs Privatized Worldwide, by Region, 1980–91

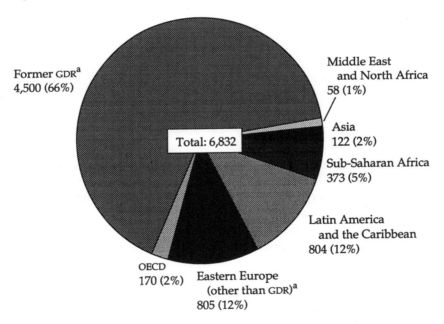

Former GDR[a]
4,500 (66%)

Middle East
and North Africa
58 (1%)

Asia
122 (2%)

Sub-Saharan Africa
373 (5%)

Total: 6,832

Latin America
and the Caribbean
804 (12%)

OECD
170 (2%)

Eastern Europe
(other than GDR)[a]
805 (12%)

Note: GDR, German Democratic Republic. Data include liquidations and any sale that reduces the government share in the firm to less than 50 percent; they exclude reprivatizations. Number in parentheses represent share of worldwide total.
a. Total may include partial (minority) sales.
Source: World Bank, Country Economics Department.

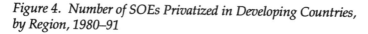

Figure 4. Number of SOEs Privatized in Developing Countries, by Region, 1980–91

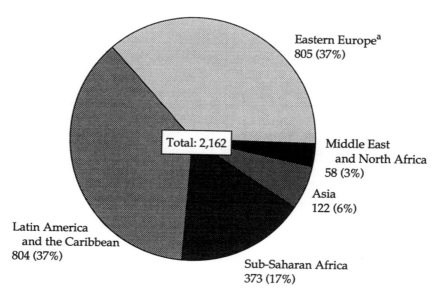

Eastern Europe[a]
805 (37%)

Middle East
and North Africa
58 (3%)

Asia
122 (6%)

Total: 2,162

Latin America
and the Caribbean
804 (37%)

Sub-Saharan Africa
373 (17%)

Note: Data include liquidations and any sale that reduces the government share in the firm to less than 50 percent; they exclude reprivatizations. Number in parentheses represent share of worldwide total.
a. Total may include partial (minority) sales.
Source: World Bank, Country Economics Department.

percent of developing country sales; close to a fifth of these occurred in Guinea.

In some developing countries, notably in Latin America, the size of the SOE sector has been substantially reduced. Starting in 1984 Mexico sold or liquidated more than 400 of its 1,155 SOEs in a wide range of sectors, including telecommunications, airlines, sugar, mining, manufacturing, and services (hotels and, more recently, banking); an additional 400 SOEs have been merged or have been transferred to municipalities. Sales have reduced total SOE assets by well over 20 percent. Chile has privatized all but 23 of its 524 SOEs since 1973, reducing ownership of producing assets from 39 percent of GDP in 1973 to 12 percent in 1989. Jamaica divested close to 20 percent of its total SOE assets, including the telephone company and hotels. Argentina and Venezuela recently sold their telephone companies and airlines and are now privatizing utilities and large industrial SOEs.

In most developing countries the aggregate effect of privatization on the relative size of the SOE sector has been modest. (But the contrast with the very high rate of creation of SOEs in the period 1960–82 is more dramatic.) One indicator of the relatively small magnitude of change is that gross proceeds from asset sales normally amount to a small proportion of GDP in comparison with the numbers of SOEs sold (figure 5). This is because the enterprises that have usually been privatized are small low-value firms in industry and services. In Guinea, for example, seventy of the ninety-eight privatizations involved the liquidation of virtually defunct retail outlets and small nonoperating enterprises.

Although large SOEs have more rarely been divested, this is changing (table 1). In the past five years alone, fourteen industrial and developing countries privatized majority ownership of twenty-two SOEs in telecommunications, power, and water supply; in a growing number of countries SOEs in these sectors are currently in the process of privatization.

The Impact of Privatization

The benefits from properly executed privatization have proved considerable, as revealed by cases in Latin America (Chile, Jamaica, and Mexico), Africa (Niger and Swaziland), and Asia (Korea and Malaysia), as well as in industrial countries (France, Japan, New Zealand, and the United Kingdom). A 1992 Bank-sponsored research project found that privatization significantly improved domestic welfare in ten of the twelve cases analyzed (box 4).[9] Productivity went up in nine of the twelve cases and stayed the same in the other three. Relaxation of the investment constraint and diversification into previously forbidden products and markets resulted in massive expansion in a number of cases.[10] Workers in the firms were not worse off after sale (even taking into account all layoffs) and in three cases were significantly better off. Buyers made money, but the other stakeholders in the process also gained. Consumers benefited or were no worse off in all but five cases.

Enterprise Performance

Other data show that privatized firms tend to exhibit higher profits, faster growth, and greater cost containment. Improved management, autonomy from political interference, and greater access to investment capital were important factors. In the United Kingdom, for example, the privatized British Telecommunications increased investment rapidly, adopted a more efficient and profit-maximizing pricing formula,[11] and

Figure 5. Privatization: Indicators of Magnitude in Selected Countries
(percent)

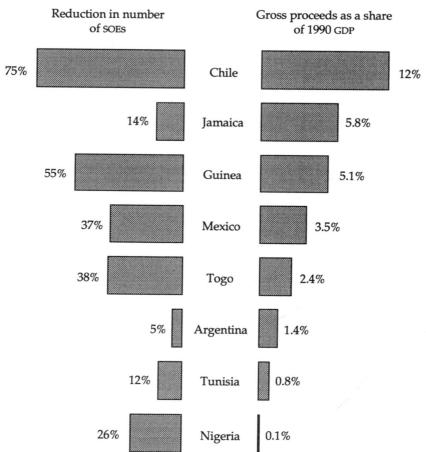

Note: Data are for 1980–91 except for Chile, 1973–91. Data include liquidations and any sale that reduces the government share in the firm to less than 50 percent; they exclude reprivatizations.
Source: World Bank, Country Economics Department.

improved productivity by eliciting greater output from a reduced work force (Galal, Jones, Tandon, and Vogelsang forthcoming).

A recent study (Megginson, Nash, and van Randenborgh 1992) of forty-one firms fully or partially privatized by public share offerings

Table 1. Recent Privatization Transactions More Than $100 Million in Value, 1988–91

Economy	Enterprise	Date	Gross transaction value (millions of dollars)	Private or public offer[a]	Sector
Mexico	Bancomer	10/91	2,550	Private	Banking
Mexico	Banamex	09/91	2,300	Private	Banking
Korea, Rep. of	Korea Electric Power	06/89	2,100	Public	Power
Venezuela	CANTV	11/91	1,885	Private	Telecommunications
Mexico	Telmex	12/90	1,760	Private	Telecommunications
Brazil	Usiminas	12/91	1,430	Private	Steel
Mexico	Mexicana de Cobre	10/88	1,360	Private	Mining
Argentina	ENTEL	11/90	1,244	Private	Telecommunications
Malaysia	Telekom Malaysia	10/90	861	Public	Telecommunications
Mexico	Cananea	09/90	475	Private	Mining
Mexico	Aerovias de México	11/88	339	Private	Airline
Philippines	Nonoc	10/90	325	Private	Mining
Taiwan (China)	China Steel	04/89	285	Public	Steel
Argentina	Aerolinas Argentinas	04/90	260	Private	Airline
Mexico	Banca Cremi	06/91	248	Private	Banking
Mexico	Multibanco de Mercantil	06/91	204	Private	Banking
Mexico	Banpaís	06/91	182	Private	Banking
Mexico	Sicartsa 1	11/91	170	Private	Steel
Chile	Compañía de Teléfonos	01/88	170	Private	Telecom
Mexico	Sidermex North	11/91	145	Private	Steel
Venezuela	VIASA	09/91	145	Private	Airline
Mexico	Mexicana de Aviacíon	06/89	140	Private	Airline
Brazil	Aracruz	05/88	130	Public	Pulp and paper
Turkey	Petkim	06/90	125	Public	Petrochemical
Hungary	Tungsram	05/89	110	Private	Electric equipment
Mexico	Nikko Hotel	10/88	110	Private	Hotel
Mexico	Tereftalos Mexicanos	11/88	106	Private	Chemical
Colombia	Papelcol	08/90	100	Private	Pulp and paper

a. Does not include sales subsequent to first transaction (for example, employee offers and international public offers) or debt-equity swap components.
Source: Privatisation International and World Bank, Country Economics Department.

Box 4. *The Welfare Consequences of Selling Public Enterprises: Case Studies from Chile, Malaysia, Mexico, and the United Kingdom*

Much of the divestiture debate has been intuitive, theoretical, and even ideological, and the effect of privatization on welfare has not been rigorously analyzed. New World Bank research on the welfare consequences of the privatization of twelve firms in Chile, Malaysia, Mexico, and the United Kingdom provides systematic and quantifiable evidence concerning the effects of privatization on the efficiency of the enterprise, on subsequent investment, and on consumer welfare. The cases cover telecommunications (three firms), airlines (four firms), electricity (two firms), a lottery company, a port, and a transport company. The research methodology captures the impact of divestiture on all important economic actors (the government, consumers, buyers of firms, workers, and competitors). Unlike many earlier analyses, it isolates the effects of privatization on firm behavior from concurrent changes in, for example, macroeconomic policy, technology, demand structure, and the regulatory framework and addresses the counterfactual question of what would have happened in the absence of divestiture.

Welfare Effects

In eleven of the twelve cases analyzed, divestiture improved domestic and world welfare; the exception was Mexicana Airlines. The magnitude of the welfare gains is substantial; the perpetual annual benefits to society in relation to predivestiture annual sales of the companies average 26 percent.*The improvements are attributable to several changes brought about by divestiture.

- The most significant change was a dramatic increase in investment. A striking example is Chile, where a local telecommunications company doubled its capacity in the five years following divestiture.
- Nine of the twelve firms showed improved productivity, thanks to better labor-management relations, improved incentives, a reduced work force, and internal reorganization.
- Output prices did not change in five cases, thanks to competition and effective regulation. Where prices did change, they overwhelmingly enhanced welfare by moving toward levels that more closely reflected scarcity values.
- Output was often diversified into activities that offered economies of scope.

(Box continues on the following page.)

Box 4 (continued)

Winners and Losers

Foreigners versus nationals. Where foreigners were involved, they did well for themselves, except in the case of Mexicana Airlines. But they were not the only winners. They also contributed to national welfare by bringing fresh capital and know-how. This is true, for example, in the case of telecommunications companies in Chile and Mexico.

Consumers. In all but five cases, consumers were either left unaffected—thanks to competition—or were considerably better off, as a result of effective regulation. For example, consumers of telecommunications services in Chile and the United Kingdom benefited substantially from divestiture.

Government versus buyers. Buyers, including many small shareholders in the United Kingdom and pension funds in Chile, came out ahead in every case except that of Mexicana Airlines. Governments lost in three cases—including two electricity companies in Chile—but only by small amounts.

Workers. Contrary to conventional wisdom, in no case in the sample did divestiture make workers of the divested firms worse off, even taking into account all layoffs and forced retirements. In three cases (Chile's electricity distribution company, ENERSIS, Mexico's Telmex, and the United Kingdom's National Freight), workers made substantial gains.

Competitors. Given the prevalence of near monopolies in the sample, divestiture had no significant effect on competitors except in Chile and Malaysia. In Chile expansion of the divested local carrier, CTC, worked to the benefit of ENTEL, the long-distance carrier. In Malaysia the divested lottery company (Sports Toto) gained at the expense of its competitors by acquiring a larger share of the market.

Note: For a full description of the methodology, analysis of the cases, and synthesis, see Galal, Jones, Tandon and Vogelsang, *The Welfare Consequences of Selling Public Enterprises: Case Studies from Chile, Malaysia, Mexico, and the UK,* Country Economics Department, Public Sector Management and Private Sector Development Division, Washington, D.C., forthcoming.

* The annual component of the perpetuity equivalent (ACPE) of the gains is calculated as the welfare gain multiplied by the discount factor divided by the annual sales of the company in the previous year. For example, if the welfare gain is $100, the discount factor 10 percent, and last year's sales $200, the ACPE equals 5 percent.

between 1981 and 1989 in fifteen countries (primarily industrial but also including Chile, Jamaica, and Mexico) shows substantial efficiency gains. Once privatized, the firms increased returns on sales, assets, and equity; improved internal efficiency by better utilization of physical and human resources; improved their capital structure, becoming less leveraged; increased capital expenditures; and marginally increased their work forces as a result of higher investments and faster growth.

In Mexico sixty-two privatized petrochemical and auto parts firms increased investments to as much as 75 percent of gross sale revenues over three years, improved their financial management, upgraded technological processes, and, in what is often a by-product of privatization in industrial and developing countries alike, reduced management numbers but paid the remainder at more competitive rates. (This occurs more rarely with workers' incentives, but wages did increase in two of the twelve cases analyzed in the Bank study described in box 4.)

Most privatization success stories come from high- or middle-income countries. In low-income settings, as discussed below, privatization is more difficult to launch, and the chances of a negative outcome are greater. Still, positive results have been obtained in several low-income countries. In Bangladesh privatized textile companies were more profitable than public sector mills. This was partly a result of debt writeoffs, but greater attention to cost containment and more aggressive marketing were also at work. Privatized mills adjusted their prices and production schedules daily or even hourly, while prices of public mills were altered only twice a year (Lorch 1988).

Privatization has in some cases led to the liquidation of nonviable firms that were being kept alive by government protection and subsidies. In Guinea, for example, only four of twenty-eight privatized firms continue to operate profitably; two others are operating close to the break-even point. Nine of the remaining enterprises never resumed operations after sale, and the remaining thirteen are in difficulty because of procurement problems, limited export markets, lack of working capital, and limited access to government subsidies and commercial credit (Suzuki 1991).

Bankruptcies and closures do not indicate that the policy was misguided. Few developing countries can afford to subsidize, at the expense of the many, the relatively small number of workers and managers in unproductive SOE jobs that, typically, pay higher-than-average wages.[12] The demise of loss-making firms, public or private, can free assets for more productive uses, eliminate a burden on the economy, and allow more productive investment—and job creation—elsewhere.

Fiscal Impact

Privatization revenues have been significant in some developing countries, particularly in Latin America, where large SOEs have been sold
(figure 6). But net revenues from SOE sales have usually been modest
because most transactions have been small, the up-front costs associated
with privatization (settlement of enterprise debt, unpaid taxes, and
transaction fees) have been high, and sales have often been on installment plans. In Guinea, for example, total assets sold amounted to 21
billion Guinean francs, of which only 2 billion were paid (as of June
1991), as a result of lengthy repayment periods and defaults by purchasers. (The use of debt to finance sales is discussed in chapter 4.) In Ghana
only 57 percent of total sale proceeds has been paid to date.

Figure 6. Gross Proceeds from Privatization, 1980–91
(millions of dollars)

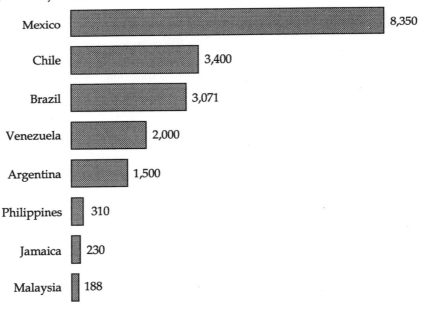

Mexico	8,350
Chile	3,400
Brazil	3,071
Venezuela	2,000
Argentina	1,500
Philippines	310
Jamaica	230
Malaysia	188

Note: Data are for 1980–91 except for Chile, 1973–91. Data include liquidations and any
sale that reduces the government share in the firm to less than 50 percent; they exclude
reprivatizations.
Source: World Bank, Country Economics Department.

Net proceeds can also be negative in the short run, but this is only a small part of the story. More important, privatization has reduced the transfer of explicit and implicit government subsidies to SOEs and has increased transfers from privatized enterprises to the government. In Mexico government transfers to SOEs at the end of 1988 were down 50 percent, a $4 billion savings from 1982, largely as a result of the stabilization program and the hard budget constraint but also because of privatization.[13] In Chile the net annual flow of funds from the privatized electricity distribution firm ENERSIS declined following divestiture because the government no longer received dividends; taxes, however, increased as enterprise performance improved over time (Galal, Jones, Tandon, and Vogelsang forthcoming). Argentina's privatized ENTel paid $100 million more in taxes in the first year after sale. And in Malaysia revenue from levies on the privatized lottery was three times greater (in real terms) than revenue from the former SOE.

Consumer Welfare

Of the twelve cases summarized in box 4, consumers were either left unaffected or were considerably better off in all but five cases. The availability and quality of products or services have often improved after privatization.[14] In the United Kingdom telecommunication consumers in the aggregate have done better every year since the announcement of sale. Consumers of long-distance service did considerably better in all years, while the position of consumers of local and other services remained more or less unchanged over the whole period. Although such factors as increased competition and technological change also played a role, new managers with full operational autonomy (within an effective regulatory framework) were critical in obtaining the gains. There was some deterioration in the quality of service in the early years after privatization, partly because of increased demand, but subsequent improvements have made current service better than before sale. In Chile paying electricity consumers are better off, but those who used to be able to get free electricity through illegal connections are worse off, since private management has cut electricity losses.[15] In Argentina, however, following the sale of telecommunications and airlines, price increases—allowed under the sales contract—provoked public complaints that led the government to pay more attention to strengthening the regulatory framework (where required) and selecting future bidders on the basis of those offering to guarantee the lowest tariffs. Even in this instance, however, the privatized telephone companies have increased the percentage of completed calls from 70 percent to close to 100 percent, reduced the number of lines out of service, and begun an ambitious program of expansion that should greatly increase the quantity and quality of service.

Support for Privatization by the World Bank Group

The World Bank Group has long assisted its borrowers' efforts to improve the performance of SOEs without changing ownership, primarily by attempting to subject public enterprises to the conditions and signals of a profit-maximizing firm operating in a competitive market. But changing perceptions and attitudes in member governments, combined with difficulties in sustaining SOE reforms and the growing body of evidence on the benefits of privatization, have created opportunities for the World Bank Group to support privatization. The complementary roles of the World Bank, the IFC, and MIGA mean that World Bank Group support adds up to more than the sum of its parts.

The World Bank

The World Bank's primary role in privatization has been to help establish an appropriate policy environment in which ownership change will produce efficiency gains; these gains, in turn, will expand production and employment and enhance welfare over the long run. Between fiscal 1981 and the first half of fiscal 1992, 182 Bank operations supported privatization in sixty-seven countries, half of them in Sub-Saharan Africa (figure 7). Bank lending for divestiture began in fiscal 1981. The number of operations escalated sharply in fiscal 1984 and then rose steadily, except for a slight dip in fiscal 1991. (Sixteen projects were approved in the first six months of fiscal 1992, compared with ten during the first half of fiscal 1991.)

Privatization has become an important part of adjustment programs: about 70 percent of all structural adjustment loans (SALs) and 40 percent of all sectoral adjustment loans (SECALs) support privatization by helping governments to develop strategies, classify candidates for sale, establish timetables for implementation, and develop an appropriate supervisory and institutional framework (figure 8). The Bank also supports financial and managerial restructuring of enterprises prior to sale (21 percent of all operations), the creation of special facilities and funds to help pay outstanding liabilities, and credit schemes to help finance privatization (13 percent).

Figure 7. World Bank–Supported Privatization Operations in Developing Countries, Fiscal 1981 through December 1991

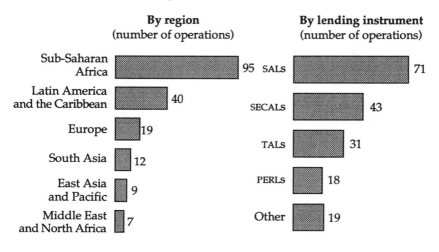

By region
(number of operations)

By lending instrument
(number of operations)

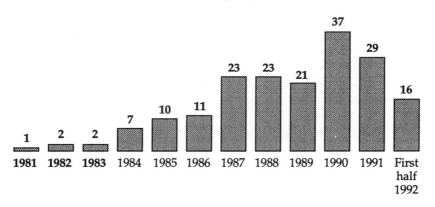

By fiscal year
(number of annual loans and credits)

Note: SALS, structural adjustment loans (including economic recovery operations; SECALS, sectoral adjustment loans; TALS, technical assistance loans (including SOE-specific technical assistance and other sector technical assistance operations); PERLS, public enterprise reform loans (including PE SECALs and PE and public sector reform operations). Other refers to hybrid and investment operations.
Source: World Bank, Country Economic Department.

Figure 8. Components of World Bank Support for Privatization, Fiscal 1981 through December 1991
(*percentage of operations with privatization component*)

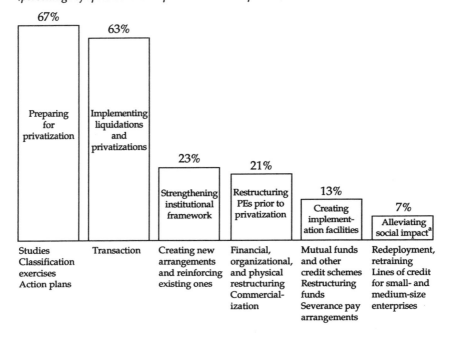

a. Excludes support for social safety nets under adjustment loans that is not explicitly linked to privatization programs.
Source: World Bank, Country Economics Department.

In addition to adjustment loans, more than sixty Bank operations finance technical assistance for privatization, mostly in Sub-Saharan Africa and in Latin America and the Caribbean. These programs support preparation, institutional strengthening, and specific transactions by financing legal or financial advisers, asset valuators, and industrial and technical consultants and specialists. A growing number of technical assistance operations also help governments develop the capacity to regulate privatized monopolies (particularly in Latin America and the Caribbean—for example, in Argentina, Mexico, and Venezuela). The Bank also assists privatizing countries to build a social safety net, usually as part of the overall adjustment program.

Bank support for privatization has produced positive results, as documented in the previous sections; a detailed case in point is presented in box 5. Two shortcomings, however, have been observed (Nellis 1989b; Kikeri 1990).

- First, the instruments used may not always have been those most appropriate for the situation. Close to two-thirds of Bank support for privatization has been in adjustment operations, especially SALs. SALs play a critical role in getting the process started and in fostering the macroeconomic policy reforms without which the supply response to and benefits of privatization would be minimal. But because of their broad scope and short time horizons, SALs alone cannot meet the longer-term specific needs of privatization—building an institutional and regulatory framework, negotiating complex and technically demanding transactions, and financing the sometimes large transitional costs from layoffs and closures. Slower-disbursing lending instruments such as hybrid investment and policy loans and technical assistance loans provide the enduring assistance that borrowers need. Increasingly, the Bank is combining SALs with other instruments that are phased in to meet borrowers' needs at different stages of the privatization process.
- Second, Bank operations have been overly specific concerning targets and deadlines for the completion of sales, and this has been counterproductive. Deadlines provide investors with an unfair bargaining advantage and can prompt hasty sales that rely too heavily on concessions and sweeteners. This problem is being addressed through flexible conditionality. Instead of requiring the sale of a particular enterprise by a particular date, the Bank is looking at more general indications of the government's commitment to privatization, such as enacting critical laws, bringing SOEs to the point of sale, creating the institutional framework, and privatizing some specified percentage of total SOE assets.

The IFC

As is true of its overall investment operations, the developmental impact of the IFC's privatization operations is reflected not so much in the number or size of individual transactions as in their ability to strengthen investor confidence. Although these operations constitute a relatively small portion of the aggregate volume of business in the countries involved, IFC analysis shows that they have succeeded in catalyzing additional flows of risk capital from foreign and local sponsors prepared to provide essential technical and management services. The focus has been on completing model privatization transactions, to facilitate the

Box 5. Assisting Privatization: The Bank's Role in Argentina

By the late 1980s Argentina's SOEs accounted for 50 percent of the total public sector deficit. In 1989 the newly elected Menem government began a massive withdrawal of the state from major productive sectors. From the outset the Bank played a key role in assisting the government to develop and execute a coherent reform strategy.

The government began with the restructuring and privatization of the three largest SOEs, comprising two-thirds of SOE employment and revenues and one-half of the SOE operating deficit: telephone (ENTel), oil, and railways. ENTel was chosen as an early case to build policy credibility; investor interest was fairly high, and Bank staff had already laid the groundwork over three years of extensive dialogue. The tight timetable included a number of demanding tasks: the breakup of industrial complexes into viable, attractive business units; demonopolization, deregulation, and development of regulatory capacity; and establishment of transparent sale conditions. Success hinged both on the availability of skilled personnel (sectoral specialists, management consultants, lawyers, and investment bankers)—the lack of which emerged as a bottleneck—and on government capacity to coordinate and manage the work of these people.

The Bank helped the government meet these challenges in a number of ways. In 1987 it initiated an intensive policy dialogue and SOE sector reviews, followed by large-scale missions and workshops to promote consensus among stakeholders and help devise a regulatory framework for the telephone monopoly. It secured loan funds of about $7 million to cover up-front technical assistance costs and fielded an interdisciplinary team of experts to advise on necessary tasks. A critical $300 million adjustment loan, combined with a technical assistance loan, supported the initial wave of reforms. Throughout, the Bank helped shape the government's program by emphasizing economic value over revenue maximization, the establishment of appropriate regulations, and the opening up of sectors to avoid monopoly concentration.

Argentina sold ENTel in November 1990. Railway and hydrocarbon restructuring is well advanced in preparation for privatization. The government has awarded a concession for a major railway cargo line. As of December 1991 gross proceeds for all sales had reached $1.5 billion in cash and $7.2 billion in debt conversion, representing 20 percent of the total commercial bank debt outstanding. Thanks to technical assistance funded with undisbursed proceeds from earlier Bank loans, water supply, power, and natural gas privatizations are also well under way. The government is pressing on with plans to privatize port infrastructure, the merchant marine fleet, and the postal service. Most recently, the Bank mobilized a Japanese grant to prepare for the sale of steel and defense industries by the end of 1993, with the support of a follow-up Bank loan.

supply response to macroeconomic reform and, in the process, to make the IFC's transactional experience available to governments that are formulating privatization policy.

The IFC's privatization transactions and fee-based advisory work complement the Bank's policy and program support. As of January 1992 the IFC had invested in twenty completed privatization transactions, and another ten had been approved by its management for appraisal during the fiscal year. The number of IFC privatization projects and the rate of approval have been increasing since 1986, the date of the first such project. Investments have been made in a variety of sectors, including development finance services, textiles, agroindustry, hotels, and iron and steel. Project size has varied from less than $5 million to more than $190 million, and the IFC's own stake (equity, loan, or both) from less than $1 million to more than $60 million. The foreign sponsors of these projects view the IFC's presence as an essential prerequisite to their own participation.

Recently, the IFC has begun offering fee-based advisory services. During the past two years the IFC has provided advice to a number of countries seeking to improve the efficiency of state-owned enterprises through partial or complete privatization. Eastern European countries have been particularly important clients in recent years; others include Argentina, Morocco, the Philippines, and Portugal. The IFC has also provided advice on the "buy" side of privatization transactions, the operational and financial structuring of projects, and corporate sectoral development strategy (box 6).

MIGA

MIGA, established in 1988, encourages foreign private direct investment in developing countries by providing long-term investment insurance (guarantees) against noncommercial risks—in particular, the risks of currency transfer, expropriation, breach of contract, and war and civil disturbance. As of early February 1992 MIGA had seventy-seven member countries; another thirty-eight are in the process of completing their membership requirements.

MIGA's involvement in privatization has so far been limited. Three of its first twenty-five projects involved privatizations; one of these, General Electric–Tungsram in Hungary, was a very large undertaking. An additional four privatization projects have already been approved by MIGA's Board and await investors' decisions; four more are currently under active consideration. Because MIGA's role is to strengthen investor confidence, its potential impact on privatization is large. This is most

---

Box 6.   IFC Advisory Services and the Privatization of Skoda Plzen

Skoda Plzen, Czechoslovakia's largest heavy industrial complex, with eighteen production divisions in related but dissimilar activities and some 38,000 employees, needed assistance in identifying and negotiating with an appropriate foreign joint-venture partner capable of transforming the company's energy and transport activities into internationally competitive businesses. The IFC, which deployed considerable staff resources for this task, initially prepared a strategic review for the company, analyzing its strengths and weaknesses and arriving at an action plan for the various product groups. The company accepted the action plans and engaged in negotiations with prospective joint-venture partners concerning six product divisions. The IFC helped Skoda in negotiating the terms and conditions of foreign participation and in structuring and drafting the definitive agreements.

Skoda and Siemens AG have now signed an agreement in principle whereby Siemens will acquire a major equity stake on the basis of a set of firm commitments regarding financial contribution, capital investment, technology transfer, market access, management, and training. The agreement will make Skoda a competitive producer and will ensure continuing employment for much of its work force.

---

evident in Eastern Europe. No less than 30 percent of MIGA's active applications for guarantees are from that area, and the great majority are prospective privatizations. MIGA has received more than twice as many applications for coverage from Poland than from any other country. MIGA's activities benefit from and complement the Bank's policy and program support, as well as the IFC's efforts.

3. Objectives and Strategy for Privatization

For privatization to have positive, enduring effects, certain elements are necessary: strong political commitment, the right macroeconomic conditions, public consensus and understanding, and transparency in the process. These prerequisites are discussed in the sections below.

Privatization is only one element—albeit a key one—in an overall strategy of private sector development and public sector reform. Experience in a range of countries, from industrial to low-income, indicates that privatization is most effectively advanced when it is part of a broader macroeconomic reform program that creates an enabling environment for efficient private enterprises and that states unambiguously the scope and methods of reform. Governments should not necessarily try to plan the privatization process down to the last detail; such attempts have regularly proved counterproductive.[16] But there is still a critical role for the state—as the owner of SOEs—in developing the strategy and principles for privatization.

Conditions for Success

Two main factors affect the strategy for privatization and the outcomes in terms of economic productivity and consumer welfare: (a) country conditions, a composite factor that takes into account the extent to which the macroeconomic policy framework is or is not market-friendly and the effectiveness of regulatory and supervisory institutions, and (b) the nature of the market into which the enterprise is divested—competitive or potentially competitive, or noncompetitive (see figure 1).[17]

Country Conditions

In countries with a market-friendly policy framework and a relatively well-developed institutional and regulatory capacity, privatization will be both easier to undertake and more likely to yield financial and economic benefits. This is true for all types of enterprises, in both competitive and noncompetitive sectors. For this reason the World Bank Group often supports privatization as one element of a broader government program of macroeconomic (trade, price, and exchange rate) and public sector reforms. Such reforms help attract private investors and make the process feasible; they also ensure that privatization will expand competition and productive efficiency rather than simply transfer rents from SOEs to new private owners. Successful privatizers such as Chile and Mexico began macroeconomic reforms well before privatization. Middle-income countries, with a better capacity to regulate, tend to be in a better position to privatize rapidly enterprises in noncompetitive sectors.

A well-functioning legal framework is especially important to successful privatization (box 7). Creating such a framework entails developing important aspects of business legislation (property law, competition law, corporate law, dispute settlement, environmental legislation, and so on), defining property rights, modifying the legislation of SOEs to be divested, and developing laws for organizing the privatization process.

Poorly managed privatization has sometimes led to unfavorable outcomes. Poor macroeconomic conditions, combined with excessive sweeteners in the terms and conditions of sale (such as new monopoly rights and overgenerous tax and duty exemptions), have reduced competition and efficiency, as, for example, in Guinea. The distributional effects of privatization have yet to be thoroughly analyzed, but the possibility that assets will be concentrated in the hands of a small elite is a legitimate concern. Sales without competitive bidding, at predetermined concessionary prices, or into a protected market have helped enrich well-connected individuals. Even when the well-connected were not given protection or a particularly discounted price, the lack of open bidding may have meant that the best-qualified people were not given an opportunity to acquire the enterprises and put them to productive use.

Privatization of both competitive and noncompetitive SOEs is more of a challenge in low-income countries. The process itself is difficult to carry out: in addition to the usual social and political obstacles to reform in general and divestiture in particular, macroeconomic distortions, thin capital markets, limited interest on the part of foreign investors, and weak legal, regulatory, and institutional capacity are likely to be acute problems in low-income countries. In Ghana, for example, staffing weaknesses in the privatization authority (combined with a lack of funding for severance pay) were a major delaying factor.

Box 7. Legal Aspects of Privatization

Legal issues permeate the whole privatization process, from preparation to implementation and follow-up. They occur primarily at two levels: the systemic level (laws, regulations, and institutions) and the transaction level (see Guislain 1992).

At the outset, existing legislation, as well as the legal status of the SOEs to be divested, must be analyzed to determine whether it allows privatization and is compatible with the government's objectives or whether it needs to be amended. Laws may need to be enacted to abolish a monopoly, regulate or deregulate the particular sector, strengthen the country's capital markets, authorize the transfer of the particular SOEs to the private sector, or organize the privatization process itself. Some SOEs may have a legal status that does not allow or facilitate divestiture, in which case a change in status (for example, corporatization) will be required. If the ownership of assets is disputed, the rights of the contending parties must be clarified. All these elements need to be addressed before privatization can start.

Lawyers will also be needed during the implementation stage to draft agreements and to advise buyer and seller on the negotiations. Advice may cover such topics as avoidance of conflicts of interest (or the appearance thereof) for government officials and advisers; confidential agreements with bidders and other parties involved in the transaction; observance of due diligence under the difficult circumstances common to many developing countries; and treatment of SOE creditors' rights.

Following completion of the privatization transaction, legal safeguards are required to ensure that all parties comply with the terms of the privatization agreements and to develop effective mechanisms to enforce compliance. The regulatory framework may need to be fine-tuned to ensure that it is fulfilling expectations by allowing the private enterprise to develop while protecting the legitimate interests of consumers, competitors, and taxpayers.

The range and complexity of legal issues that could arise in privatization programs are almost endless. In each country and for each transaction, privatizing governments should retain the services of qualified, experienced, and independent lawyers to help them with the identification of critical legal issues and promising solutions.

Despite the difficulties in managing the process, countries have achieved economic gains from privatization even in the most challenging settings. In Niger, one of the poorest African economies, the shift from 100 percent public to 75 percent private ownership revived a near-dead textile company. The company now operates profitably—at close to full capacity and with an increased number of employees—exports much of its production, and has won a large domestic market share against imports. Putting a clear majority of shares in the hands of the private technical partner brought about this achievement. The IFC-supported privatization of a development finance corporation in Swaziland is another major success: the firm was closed down prior to restructuring and privatization, but its profits in its second year of private ownership were better than anticipated. The 1986 privatization of an agroindustrial SOE in Mozambique led to profitability rates of more than 55 percent of sales; the privatized firm diversified into new products, began servicing its debts, and increased production fivefold. These beneficial privatizations were not easy to accomplish, but they produced results. It is the task of governments and the agencies assisting them—including the World Bank Group—to structure the enabling environment and the transactions in such a way that the potential of privatization is fulfilled.

Competitive versus Noncompetitive Enterprises

Privatization of enterprises that produce tradables in competitive or potentially competitive sectors such as industry, airlines, agriculture, and retail operations is easier than privatization in noncompetitive sectors and is likely to yield solid and rapid economic benefits (as many of the above examples indicate) as long as there are not economywide distortions that hinder competition. In countries with a favorable environment, domestic and external competition prevents monopolistic behavior and provides incentives for efficiency; here, successful privatization requires little more than adequate attention to transparency. Even in countries with an unfavorable environment, privatization can have the benefit of reducing the fiscal burden of SOE subsidies and exposing fully the costs of the distortions. In such circumstances, maximum gains can be had by rapidly privatizing competitive enterprises while undertaking trade and price liberalization and strengthening the institutional and regulatory framework.

In any developing country setting, privatization of SOEs that operate as natural monopolies—for example, in power, water supply, and telecommunications—is more difficult than privatization of firms in competitive markets: the enterprises are larger, the stakes are higher, foreign investment issues are even more salient, and capital markets are thin. Nonetheless, privatization of noncompetitive enterprises has yielded benefits in middle-income countries such as Chile, Malaysia, and Mexico—where the policy environment was favorable and the government had the capacity to implement a new or existing regulatory regime. It is in countries with market-unfriendly policies and limited private sector interest that privatization of utilities and other natural monopolies is especially difficult; divestiture of noncompetitive enterprises in settings in which capacity to regulate is low is likely to have an adverse impact on consumer welfare.

In circumstances that are not conducive to privatization, particularly in lower-income countries, privatizing management through management contracts, leases, and concessions is a step in the right direction. Greater attention should also be paid to developing competition, wherever possible, by eliminating barriers to entry and enacting appropriate regulations and to enhancing the productivity and efficiency of SOEs. Colombia, for example, changed its regulations to permit open competition between public and private operators in ports, dismantled the monopoly of the shipping cargo line, and allowed the private sector to provide rail transport services. Even where monopolies are retained, competitive activities (such as value added services, cellular services, and equipment production in telecommunications) can be spun off, and services provided in-house can be competitively bid. For example, in Venezuela a private company collects tariffs for the public water company; in Thailand the Petroleum Authority leases cars and drivers under competitive contract.

Successful privatization of noncompetitive SOEs requires a regulatory framework that separates out potentially competitive activities, sets out the tariff regime, establishes universal service goals, develops cost minimization targets, and creates a regulatory agency to supervise the established procedures. Such a framework clarifies the rules of the game and creates a stable and predictable operating environment for private investors. It also helps overcome equity concerns and political opposition by allowing decisionmakers to point to mechanisms erected to defend transparency, competition, and the public interest. In Chile, for example, the existence of a well-developed regulatory framework prior to privatization of the power companies ensured that divestiture led to increased efficiency without harming consumer interests.[18] These choices and recommended courses of action are summarized in figure 1, above.

Defining Objectives

Governments privatize SOEs for many reasons—to improve efficiency, generate revenue, disperse ownership, and develop capital markets. These goals may and often do conflict; attempts to accomplish multiple objectives can result in failure to achieve any. Government's strategic task is to balance conflicting objectives.

Enhancing efficiency should be the number one goal. Privatization has its greatest impact on economic welfare when the efficiency objective is kept in the forefront. Privatization should be used to increase competition and ensure against monopolistic behavior. The high risks and uncertainties in developing countries sometimes make prospective investors argue for special privileges and protection in exchange for private investment. But this argument is wrong and can lead to perverse results. For example, a loss-making steel mill in Togo was leased to a private firm in 1984. The conditions of the lease agreement included a high level of nominal protection (40 percent) combined with import and export duty exemptions, a favorable pricing agreement, and a low lease fee—with the government servicing the substantial debt. This deal was questionable in economic terms.[19] The government could not face closing a loser, but this "solution" simply shifted the burden—and even then only a part of it—from the budget to consumers.

Opportunities for competition exist even in sectors once regarded as naturally monopolistic. For example, U.K. water supply and electricity generation companies were broken up into, respectively, ten and sixteen independent units prior to sale. The power generation companies compete directly, while the performance of a water company in one geographic area can be compared with those in other regions to encourage what is called "yardstick competition." These sales contrast with other U.K. privatizations in which revenue maximization, not competition, was the main objective (box 8).

Maximizing short-term government revenues should not be the primary consideration. It can lead to deals that are bad for the economy (although perhaps good for the budget)—for example, the sale of competitive or potentially competitive SOEs as monopolies in order to raise the selling price and thus revenues. For infrastructural SOEs a monopoly concession may be unavoidable in some activities because of economies of scale. But the economy will be best off if the government first deregulates potentially competitive activities and establishes adequate tariff regulation and then privatizes—even if that means a lower sale price. Jamaica, for instance, privatized its telephone company with a twenty-five-year concession on local and competitive international services and with a guaranteed rate of return arrangement that exceeded industry norms and provided few incentives to reduce costs. The underlying objective in granting these sweeteners was to maximize the selling price and the

---

Box 8.   Competition and Privatization of Nontradables in the United Kingdom

In any privatization, the greater the degree of competition produced, the greater the likelihood that efficiency will be enhanced. Critics of the early experience with privatization in the United Kingdom argue that privatization could have led to greater economic benefits had monopolies in potentially competitive sectors—such as British Telecommunications, British Airways, and British Gas—been broken up into smaller competing and comparable units before sale. They were sold intact partly because the government considered that a breakup would have been costly and would have delayed privatization.

The government did promote competition by licensing Mercury Communications to compete with British Telecommunications and British Midlands to compete with British Airways, but these were small firms that were thought likely to capture only small market shares—as has indeed been the case so far. To break up the monopolies now that they have already been granted is far more difficult, since that would affect the sales price of the remaining government shares. Nevertheless, the telecommunications regulator, OFTEL, is considering a recommendation to the Monopolies and Mergers Commission that British Telecommunications be broken into competitive parts.

---

short-term revenue to government; their effect on efficiency has yet to be estimated. By contrast, in the recent telecommunications sales in Argentina, Mexico, and Venezuela, nonbasic services were opened up to varying degrees of competition. Private purchasers obtained seven-to-ten-year concessions in local services, but the deals were combined with incentives that encouraged expansion and cost reduction. For example, the privatized Telmex will pay a corporate tax rate of 10 percent if it meets the promised investment schedule and 29 percent if it does not. In this instance, as in many other infrastructure sales, greater weight was given to follow-on investments than to price.

Privatization can help develop capital markets (and vice versa), but capital market development should not be an objective of privatization. In many countries privatization has helped develop and expand financial markets. Chile, France, Jamaica, Japan, Nigeria, and the United Kingdom increased the number of shareholders and total market capitalization as a result of privatization (table 2). Yet an overemphasis on stock market sales can cause problems in developing countries. Where absorptive capacity is weak in relation to the size of individual or total sales, the

Table 2.   *Privatization and Capital Market Development*

Country	Number of enterprises sold through stock exchange	Proceeds of sales through stock exchange (millions of dollars)[a]	Proceeds as a percent-age of stock market capi-talization[b]	Number of new shareholders
Canada[c]	2	812.0	0.4	n.a.
Chile (since 1985)	14	893.5	9.3	63,316[d]
France	14	5,148.1	3.0	5,000,000
Jamaica	3	120.8	12.6	30,000
Japan	1	76,500.0	1.7	1,670,000
Nigeria	16	27.0	2.0	400,000
Trinidad and Tobago	2	6.8	2.5	n.a.
Tunisia	2	8.6	n.a.	n.a.
United Kingdom	14	51,720.5	6.0	7,400,000

a. Includes share auctions and public offerings.
b. Market capitalization in year of last public offering.
c. Includes only federal ("Crown") enterprises.
d. Does not include shareholders in ENDESA.
Source: For Chile, France, Jamaica, and the United Kingdom, Bouin and Michalet 1991; for Canada, Nigeria, Trinidad and Tobago, and Tunisia, World Bank, Country Economics Department; for Japan, Takano 1992.

result can be delays and the crowding out of new private share issues. The sale of 24 percent of Telekom Malaysia in September 1990, for example, aimed at raising 2.35 billion ringgit, compared with a total of 3 billion ringgit raised on the Kuala Lumpur stock exchange in 1989. In Nigeria, where new private offerings in 1989 totaled 800 million naira, 3 billion naira were expected to be raised from privatizations between 1990 and 1991.

A key lesson of experience is that it takes time to develop appropriate institutions and regulations in weak capital markets. Privatizing poorly performing enterprises without information and prudential regulation may exploit small first-time investors, and if an improperly investigated sale goes bad, it can lead to pressure for government bailouts or call into question the credibility of future sales. Where capital markets are weak and prudential regulation poor, stock market sales are not an immediate option. Other sale mechanisms such as sale of assets and joint ventures can and should be used.

The volatility of developing country stock markets can set back privatization. In Korea, for example, a 1990 attempt to sell shares in three commercial banks attracted 3.5 million would-be investors, but the market fell 50 percent before payment came due, and only 200 investors actually paid. The damage to the overall privatization program was severe. Moreover, in most developing countries the majority of SOEs are poor performers and are unsuitable for stock market offerings. Preparing them for public offering involves time and resources that are better spent on infrastructure or on investments in human resources that benefit a larger part of society. Finally, as discussed in chapter 4, capital market transactions involve potentially large pricing discounts that can result in a political backlash against privatization.

Widely dispersed ownership should not interfere with improved corporate governance. A proven way to improve corporate governance is to turn SOEs over to private owners with enough of a stake to benefit from improved performance (or to suffer from a deterioration) and with the power to achieve results. But this conflicts with another frequently proposed distributional objective of divestiture, the promotion of wide share ownership. Although over time, share ownership tends to reconcentrate,[20] many governments (Chile, France, Jamaica, Nigeria, and the United Kingdom, for example) see wide distribution of shares as an important benefit of privatization. When ownership of firms is widely dispersed, management performance tends to be sacrificed. In industrial countries with mature stock markets, management discipline can to some extent be provided through the threat of corporate takeovers and bankruptcy, influential financial journalism, and the active participation of nonexecutive directors. (Even under these circumstances, however, the lack of managerial accountability can be a problem.) In developing countries that lack these conditions, strong private management and control are essential for turning around troubled SOEs.

One way to both improve corporate governance and spread ownership is to reserve core shareholdings (at least temporarily) for strategic investors committed to the company. This was a key strategy in Chile's second privatization phase. In France, prior to the public offering of shares, 15 to 30 percent of equity was offered to core investors at premium prices (2.5 to 10 percent above market price). The benefit of the core investor approach is that it puts skilled owner-investors in charge of the assets; the obvious risk is the creation of entrenched interests. Mexico, in privatizing its partially state-owned banks, attempted to resolve the dilemma by giving incentives to core investors but requiring them to divest a portion of their shares after an initial period. In Venezuela banks were sold to private investors with the provision that shares would be offered more widely to the public and employees over a three-to-five-year period.

Another way is to involve institutional investors, such as life insurance, pension, and provident funds. Although institutional investors tend to be more passive than trade owners, often exerting limited influence or control in direct corporate governance, they can temporarily substitute when trade buyers are lacking (as is proposed in Eastern Europe and Central Asia; see chapter 5). They are preferable to a large number of dispersed shareholders, since they tend to watch dividends more carefully and to sell shares if income stagnates or falls. This exit can have a positive supervisory effect on management or at least assist hostile takeovers.

In short, the goal of efficiency should be kept in the forefront. Short-term revenue generation, development of capital markets, and dispersion of ownership can be important considerations, but they should not be the primary goals of privatization.

What, How Much, and How Fast to Sell

Once objectives are clarified, strategic decisions need to be made about the scope and pace of privatization. The early 1980s witnessed much debate about what should be sold. Airlines, petrochemical plants, and cement and steel mills were often defined as "strategic" and thus unfit for privatization. Today, government thinking has changed, and virtually all SOEs are being opened up to privatization.

Most divesting governments—including Chile, Jamaica, Mexico, the Philippines, Poland, Togo, and the United Kingdom—began by giving priority to small and medium-size firms in competitive sectors. Such sales are simple and quick: they require little prior restructuring and institutional capacity, entail minimal political risk, and, since they are more easily absorbed by local private investors, reduce the thorny issue of foreign ownership. Speed is essential to help put assets to more productive use and to remove the managerial and financial burden on the government. Experience with small sales helps prepare privatizers for subsequent sales of larger, more complex SOEs.[21] To ensure credibility, close attention needs to be paid to the development of an announcement of privatization, clear procedures for bidding, and a timetable for sale.

A few governments, including those of Argentina and Brazil, have nonetheless given priority to the privatization of large SOEs. Such sales are complex and time-consuming, especially if they involve utilities or other nontradables; they require the development of a competitive environment and regulatory framework, sophisticated financial engineering, and sensitive labor restructuring. But there can be compelling reasons for adopting this strategy. First, the window of political opportunity may be but briefly open, and the most important cases are best tackled before circumstances change. Second, large privatizations provide instant policy credibility and send clear signals of government commitment to financial markets and investors. Third, the potential economic and financial benefits may be worth the risks. Privatizing badly managed firms that provide critical upstream goods and services (telecommunications and power, for example) helps accelerate modernization and growth and removes constraints on private sector development. Privatizing a few large loss-makers can have an enormous budgetary impact; in Argentina, for example, the three SOEs on which the government focused first—telephones, railways, and oil—accounted for 50 percent of the SOE operating deficit.

Priorities for privatization are country-specific. In the end, the choice depends on investor interest, government capacity, and the sectors and enterprises most in need of new investments and efficiency improvements. Surprisingly, a number of serious loss-makers have been successfully sold early in the process. Most of the IFC's privatization transactions, for example, involved SOEs that were either closed or were making recurrent losses. Most of the companies required investments for modernization, and privatization provided access to private investment capital.

Privatizing Management

Sales have a big advantage over nonownership methods of privatization, since they transfer property rights to profit-oriented owners who push their companies to perform better, at lower cost, and to pay more attention to the needs and demands of clients. But outright sales may not be financially or politically feasible in some country and enterprise circumstances, and alternative ways of improving SOE efficiency and involving the private sector often need to be explored.

Significant gains can be realized by bringing in aggressive private managers and allowing the SOE to operate like a private firm, even if ownership of assets is not transferred. Management contracts, leases (or *affermage*), and concession arrangements are particularly useful. They can help facilitate later sales in activities to which it is difficult to attract private investors and in low-income countries where capital markets and domestic private sectors are weak, an unfavorable policy framework makes private investors reluctant to take on ownership of large assets in need of modernization (railways, water, power, and the like), or capacity to regulate is poor.

In *management contracts*, the government pays a private company a fee for managing the SOE. Management contracts are common in hotels, airlines, and agriculture, where considerable experience has routinized contract negotiation and monitoring and an ample supply of experienced managers is available. They have been less frequent in the industrial sector, although Sri Lanka employed private management contractors to turn around three loss-making textile firms and prepare them for privatization. (All three firms were subsequently sold.)

Management contracts are usually less politically contentious than sales. They avoid the risk of asset concentration and can enhance productivity. Governments nonetheless tend to prefer sales, for a number of reasons. Typically, contractors do not assume risk; operating losses must be borne by the owner (the state) even though it has relinquished day-to-day control of the operation. Many standard management contracts are flat fee-for-service arrangements, payable regardless of profits, and so provide little incentive to improve efficiency. Furthermore, management contracts are time-consuming to develop and can be expensive to implement. Unless proper legal safeguards are developed and are enforced by monitoring, there is a risk that the contractor may run down the assets. Another drawback is that few management contractors provide adequate training for local counterparts (Hegstad and Newport 1987). These risks can be reduced with properly drawn-up contracts, but that requires strengthening the government's capacity to negotiate, monitor, and enforce contractual obligations.

Leases overcome some of the drawbacks of management contracts. The private party, which pays the government a fee to use the assets, assumes the commercial risk of operation and maintenance and thus has greater incentives (and obligations) to reduce costs and maintain the long-term value of the assets. Fees are usually linked to performance and revenues. Lease arrangements have been widely used in Africa, particularly in sectors to which it is difficult to attract private investors: examples include steel and petroleum refining in Togo, water supply in Guinea and Côte d'Ivoire, electricity in Côte d'Ivoire, road transport in Niger, port management in Nigeria, and mining operations in Guinea (Triche 1990). In each case the contracted firm is a joint foreign-local enterprise, with the foreign partner bringing in essential technical and managerial expertise. Leases usually contain built-in incentives to reduce costs; in Côte d'Ivoire, for example, the leased water company reduced the number of high-paid expatriate staff from forty to twelve. Technical efficiency, new connections, and billing and collection of receivables also improved dramatically (box 9).

Box 9. *Private Management of Water Supply in Côte d'Ivoire*

Private management of Côte d'Ivoire's water supply has improved efficiency. But the experience also reveals the limitations of management contracts and leases as long-run substitutes for private ownership and good regulatory policies.

Thirty years ago, the third largest French water utility (SAUR) created an Ivorien subsidiary, the Côte d'Ivoire Water Distribution Company (SODECI). In 1960 SODECI won its first competitive bid to operate and maintain Abidjan's water supply system. Under a mix of *affermage* (lease) and management and concession contracts, it gradually added to its portfolio the management of sewerage and drainage systems and small urban and rural water supply systems throughout the country. In 1978 the company's shares began trading on the Ivorien stock market. Private Ivoriens now hold 46 percent of its share capital, with SAUR retaining 46 percent, employees 5 percent, and the state 3 percent.

Thanks to the technical and managerial expertise of its foreign partner and the strong contractual incentives to cut costs, SODECI achieved remarkable results in urban areas. By the late 1980s water losses had been cut to 12 percent and the collection rate had been raised to 98 percent for private consumers. At 130 water connections per employee, labor productivity was twice that of the next-best West African water utility. Moreover, the number of expatriate staff has declined from forty to twelve.

Despite SODECI's good record, overall performance in the water sector fared poorly because of the government's investment and pricing policies. For example, the government discriminated against urban industrial consumers to subsidize rural investments and insisted that free connections be provided for targeted urban groups. Over a brief period tariffs were doubled for industrial consumers, curbing their production and thus reducing job opportunities. Overinvestment led to underutilized capacity—50 percent in Abidjan and 28 percent in other urban areas—and a breakdown in sector finances. In the mid-1980s the government attempted to sell to SODECI the water supply infrastructure that it manages (and the associated debts), but the company lacked sufficient capital to purchase the assets. In 1988 the government granted SODECI a further concession for urban water supply. Unlike the previous *affermage* relationship, this contract for the first time makes the company responsible for financing future investments in urban water supply. SODECI's experience shows that privatization of management is a good beginning but is only a temporary solution in sectors in which the government controls prices and investment policies.

Concessions go further; the holder has responsibility for capital expenditures and investments (unlike a lessee). In general, concessions are more desirable but less feasible than leases. This is so because private financing (or willingness) tends to be weak in comparison with the size of the investment, particularly in sectors or countries in which the political and economic risks are seen to be high. In such instances the government might have to assume responsibility for planning and investment. Concessions have been successfully used in the recent privatizations of telecommunications and railways in Argentina. Venezuela plans to grant private firms concessions to operate and finance investments in ports and water supply.

Few systematic analyses of the experience with private management arrangements have been done. What evidence there is shows the importance of avoiding government interference in management. Instead, managers should be held accountable for results and given incentives to improve operations and increase the long-term value of the assets.[22] Some ways of providing incentives are to link fees to enterprise performance, encourage equity investments, or give managers the option to purchase some or all of the assets or shares on expiration of the contract or lease. This last method must not link market value at the end of the lease period with purchase price, or the lessee will have an incentive to run down the value of the enterprise.

Private management arrangements have their utility, and they can and should be used when immediate privatization is not chosen. But because change in ownership is eventually needed to lock in performance gains, private management arrangements are likely to work best as a step toward full privatization. Political authorities often give private managers and contractors the power to turn around poorly performing enterprises, but over time, particularly if and as SOE earnings improve, the temptation to interfere reasserts itself. Furthermore, privatizing management usually does not bring the increased investment that can be a major accomplishment of ownership change (as in the cases described in box 4). In some few instances, such as the Guinea water project, privatization of management can be combined with World Bank lending for expansion of infrastructure. This approach has advantages over direct investment in an SOE, but experience shows that it can run into problems (see box 9).

Full versus Partial Sale

Sales of minority shares can have positive effects on efficiency provided that managerial control is transferred to competent core investors and the government's voting rights are limited so as to curtail day-to-day interference. Some countries have started out by selling minority shares. In Chile shares of large and "sensitive" enterprises were sold gradually to investors until the state retained just over 50 percent. This was followed by an offer of 2 or 3 percent, which left the government in a minority position. The remaining shares were then sold quickly.

Minority sales are particularly beneficial when competition is introduced, management is strengthened, and the minority share offering is a prelude to a majority share offering at a later stage, thus ensuring autonomy. In Japan Nippon Telegraph and Telephone (NTT) recorded large financial and efficiency gains after 33 percent of its shares were sold to 1.6 million small shareholders (with a further government commitment to sell up to 67 percent of total shares). The NTT was at the same time exposed to competition, and a new chief executive officer (CEO) from the private sector was appointed. As a result, profits rose in spite of reductions in long-distance tariffs, the staff was reduced by 20 percent in the five years after the privatization, and the quality of service improved. The NTT case, however, also points to the limits of partial privatization. A majority of shares still remains in government hands, and the NTT's corporation law allows the government to intervene in company operations—in some areas, even more than it could when the NTT was state owned. For example, the regulatory ministry can approve or reject appointments to the senior executive corps, even after such appointments have been approved by the shareholders' meeting; the ministry has also obtained the authority to approve or reject the NTT's business plan.[23]

4. Implementation

Preparing for Sale

Should enterprises be restructured prior to sale, and, if so, how and when? There is a significant difference between (a) legal, organizational, managerial, financial, and labor-restructuring measures, which involve no new investments, and (b) large new investments for plant modernization or rehabilitation.

For small and medium-size competitive SOEs that can be sold through competitive bidding, there are few financial or economic gains to be had from any type of restructuring. Such SOEs should be sold "as is," at the best price possible, as quickly as possible. (The choice of sale technique depends on enterprise circumstances and government objectives—see box 10.) The costs of delay are high, including potential deterioration of assets, loss of investor interest, and opportunities for opposition to coalesce. Chile, Jamaica, and Mexico successfully divested dozens—and Czechoslovakia, the former German Democratic Republic, and Poland thousands—of small companies without any prior restructuring. Firms that do not meet the market test of viability should be closed down. Liquidation does not necessarily mean the complete death of the firm; it usually puts assets to productive use in private hands. Attempts to sell nonviable firms as going concerns can create delays, jeopardize the credibility of privatization, and lead to special protection and subsidies or to subsequent government bailouts.

In large enterprises and monopolies, however, restructuring—legal, organizational, and managerial changes, financial workouts, and labor shedding—is often a necessary prelude to sale. (Such sales are also best preceded by the development of a competitive environment and appropriate regulatory framework, as discussed in chapter 3.) For reasons discussed below, new investments should be avoided once a decision to privatize an enterprise is taken.

Make organizational and managerial changes. In many cases, changes in the legal status and structure of the SOE need to be effected prior to sale.[24]

Box 10. Sale Techniques

In developed countries 90 percent of all privatizations to date have involved private sales or public share offerings. In many developing countries, however, privatizations have largely been through liquidation followed by sale of the assets. This is because most of the affected enterprises so far have been small and nonviable. Larger firms in need of reorganization are more likely to be sold through direct negotiations, competitive bidding, joint ventures, or the sale of a core shareholding to a strategic investor.

Despite their political appeal, public share offerings have seldom been used in developing countries because capital markets are shallow and SOEs are in such poor condition as to be unfit for stock market flotation. There are exceptions. Shares of well-known and profitable SOEs (financial institutions and telecommunications companies) have been successfully sold through the stock market in Chile, Jamaica, Nigeria, and the Philippines. Some larger SOEs badly in need of capital and restructuring have also issued shares to raise funds for modernization; this strategy was adopted in Tunisia (textiles), Pakistan (gas pipeline), and Mexico (airlines). The government receives no proceeds from the share issue, but its shares become more valuable thanks to the new investment and can be sold later at a higher price.

Restructuring might also involve the breakup of large firms and monopolies into viable and nonviable units, the separation of competitive from noncompetitive activities, and the identification of peripheral assets (such as real estate holdings, sports teams, restaurants, and so on) that can be sold as separate concerns. The extreme case is in Eastern Europe: in June 1990 the former German Democratic Republic had about 10,000 large and medium-size enterprises to divest; by November 1991 it had sold 4,500—but it still had about 8,000 firms to deal with because of the breakup of giant conglomerates into smaller units. Argentine authorities are breaking up the state railway company into more viable and marketable units, and Mexico did the same in the case of steel.

New managers—preferably from the private sector—with different attitudes and approaches, increased autonomy, and a commitment to privatization are key elements for success. They were critical to successful privatizations in Chile (power), Mexico (telecommunications), Venezuela (telecommunications and airlines), the United Kingdom (telecommunications and airlines), and New Zealand (telecommunications). New managers launch the process of transition from a government-run to a business operation by identifying and cutting fat and waste, showing workers and managers what it will take to run the company commercially, and demonstrating to buyers the potential of the undertaking.

Clean up enterprise liabilities. SOEs, particularly in developing countries, are typically encumbered by large debts; many have negative net worth. Private buyers have made it clear that they do not want to take on these debts, even when the sale price is discounted by the amount of the debt. They seek an immediate positive cash flow to reduce their risk and help finance new expenditures. Debt write-down is thus standard practice for divesting governments the world over.[25] The extent of the writeoff varies from case to case, but in principle the aim should be to leave the new owners with just enough capital to enable them to protect and increase the capital. The governments of Argentina and Venezuela assumed debts of $930 million and $471 million, respectively, prior to sale of their telephone companies. In Ghana the government assumed $6.3 million in debts and unpaid taxes before divestiture. In the former German Democratic Republic the government had assumed, as of November 1991, 70 percent of the old debts of the 4,500 or so companies sold.

In large SOEs with tangled financial histories, sale proceeds seldom cover all outstanding liabilities. Sorting out who is owed what and who will be repaid what (both prior to and after the transaction) is essential, but it can be complex and is often a major cause of delay in completing transactions. For example, in Tunisia, where proceeds from divestiture covered about 45 percent of the liabilities of the companies sold, under the law priority was given to reimbursing payments to the Social Security Fund (workers' pensions), and the claims of the Tunisian banking system on the enterprises greatly exceeded the remaining funds. Because, however, the government had a senior tax claim on enterprise revenues, it was able to force the banks to accept a 50-50 split of the remaining proceeds (for any debt that was not government-guaranteed). All this was time consuming and arduous but had to be done in order for the sales to go through.

Many SOEs have significant potential environmental liabilities that need to be addressed prior to sale. This issue is particularly germane in Eastern Europe and Central Asia. The cleanup of inappropriately disposed waste can be done prior to sale or can be undertaken by the purchaser as a condition of sale. Arguments can be made for or against the notion that private enterprises are less polluting than SOEs (see box 11).

Deal directly and quickly with excess labor. SOE workers are wary of privatization; they fear dismissal either before or after sale. They have

---

Box 11.   *Does Privatization Increase or Decrease Industrial Pollution?*

Although there is no hard evidence comparing how much state-owned enterprises and privately owned enterprises contribute, respectively, to industrial pollution, a circumstantial case can be made that privatization is beneficial to the environment.

- SOEs tend to use older, more-polluting technology than do private firms. Given most developing countries' inability to finance modernization investments and in light of the considerable evidence that a common effect of ownership change is increased investment, privatization should be associated with less pollution as new owners install cleaner technology.
- SOEs may more easily avoid compliance with pollution controls because they have less of an adversarial relationship with the public sector. The high levels of pollution in the centrally planned economies in Eastern Europe and the former U.S.S.R. suggest that SOEs are not more, and perhaps much less, accountable than private enterprises.
- Many SOEs receive exemptions from the pollution regulations of their owners, the government. In the United States publicly owned water treatment plants are the most consistent violators of pollution regulations.
- SOEs have tended to benefit from protection and, like other protected industries in developing countries, have tended to be more materials-intensive, more energy-intensive, and thus more pollution-intensive than private industries might have been. Without protection, such pollution-intensive industries as petrochemicals and cement might not be economically viable in some developing countries. Evidence from Latin America confirms that industrial pollution has grown more slowly in open than in closed or protected economies.

It can also be argued that privatization could increase pollution.

- Private enterprises may have more incentive to undertake polluting activities than complacent SOEs that do not have to worry if they make losses. Often SOEs leave idle valuable assets that private owners would exploit. (An example is the large amount of land in central Bangkok belonging to SOEs.)
- Private enterprises may be more likely to bribe regulators in order to evade pollution controls. They are more likely to have the money than SOEs, and they may not have the scruples of the publicly employed manager (witness their readiness to evade taxes in many countries.

(Box continues on the following page.)

Box 11 (continued)

• Private enterprises are better able to hide information from the government than are SOEs; this makes it more difficult for regulators to control them.

Clearly, ownership is no safeguard: there are reasons to fear both public and private polluters. The lesson is that governments should put in place strong and sound environmental regulations and apply them equally to public and private enterprises.

reason to be concerned, for privatization often provides the impetus for making overdue employment reforms. In Argentina, Japan, Mexico, New Zealand, Tunisia, the United Kingdom, and other countries, sales have been accompanied by the downsizing of the labor force. It is not surprising, therefore, that workers and labor unions are among the most vocal opponents of privatization, causing governments to delay or postpone privatization (as in Bangladesh, India, Sri Lanka, and Thailand). Because of the sensitivities, and despite the potential delays involved, large-scale labor shedding is best handled by the state prior to sale. This strategy is particularly applicable to large and visible firms, highly unionized activities, and mature industries such as steel. It is also obviously applicable where liquidation precedes privatization. In theory, the decision to retain or dismiss labor would appear to be best left to the new private investors: they, presumably, will be in a better position to judge what kinds of skills the firm needs, and they have the incentive to minimize severance costs. In practice, however, private investors are seldom willing to deal with potentially messy, highly visible labor disputes, and layoffs are thus best done by the state. Moreover, the government is better able to design measures to alleviate the social costs through retraining, severance pay, unemployment insurance, and other elements of the social safety net.

Some governments have sold large firms with their labor forces intact, in the interest of speed. This strategy has sometimes worked well, particularly in high-growth industries that are able to absorb presently excess labor, but problems arise where the new owners have not been given full flexibility in labor decisions. Labor restrictions reduce investor interest (as in Pakistan, where twelve-month restrictions on layoffs were in place), invite demands for subsidies or concessions to cover costs (as in the case of the jute mills in Bangladesh), and are not easily enforced. In Turkey, for instance, the sale contract for a catering company included a provision against firings. The company reportedly did not comply, but went unpunished. In Germany the selling agency, the *Treuhandanstalt*, places employment maintenance clauses in the sales contracts, with stiff monetary penalties for failure to comply. But enforcement is difficult, especially since the monitoring party—the *Treuhand* itself—is working its way out of existence as fast as possible. In at least one case a purchaser laid off staff, claiming that changes in market conditions excused him from honoring the contract, and the claim was accepted.

The employment restructuring issue is important and sensitive, and it generates much heated debate. Yet several important points are often overlooked.

First, layoffs are often necessary to improve the efficiency of SOEs, whether or not a change of ownership is involved.[26]

Second, labor opposition has been muted when employees understood that the alternative to privatization was liquidation and the general public understood the costs of continued inaction. Public awareness campaigns were critical in explaining the costs and benefits of privatization—and of the alternatives—in Japan, New Zealand, Tunisia, and Venezuela.

Third, in growing sectors surplus labor has been absorbed by new capital investments and more productive use of existing assets (telecommunications sales in Latin America and hotel sales in the Philippines and Tunisia are examples). In many documented cases, as in Chile and the United Kingdom, employment levels have risen after privatization as a result of dynamic expansion; in the Mexican auto parts industry employment rose by 30 percent (see also box 4, above). This has been true even in low-income countries. Following sale, a formerly moribund textile firm in Niger expanded its blue-collar work force and hired many more Nigerien designers, foremen, accountants, and managers.

Fourth, the private sector offers the possibility of increased salaries for those who remain employed, since wages are more likely to be tied to productivity. In Malaysia, for example, the promise of performance-based pay led almost all of the 900 employees of the Port Kelang Container Terminal to accept employment with the privatized company rather than a generous severance package or an offer of employment with the Port Authority (Leeds 1988).

Fifth, attractive severance packages have helped limit opposition and have created a social safety net. Dismissed workers benefited from severance packages that exceeded the benefits required by law in many countries. In some cases generous severance packages have induced so many voluntary departures that there has been little need for outright dismissals. In Tunisia 90 percent of redundancies were voluntary departures or early retirements; only 10 percent were outright layoffs. In Pakistan those opting for increased severance packages will get five months of their last-drawn basic salary for each year of service (one month is the minimum provided by law); this is expected to help garner labor support and provide an adequate social safety net.

Severance pay represents a transitional cost, and to the extent that it allows enterprises to shift expenditures to more productive uses, constitutes an economically productive investment.[27] Although in most instances severance costs are financed by sale proceeds, some governments have had problems in financing large amounts of severance pay, and it has sometimes become an obstacle to privatization (see box 12).

Finally, employee ownership schemes can be used to elicit support for privatization.[28] Research shows that they can also enhance productivity, although profit sharing and bonus schemes are more powerful incentives (Lee 1991). Many governments reserve a block of shares—ranging from 5 to 20 percent—for employees at reduced prices and easy credit terms. (Higher levels of employee ownership can lead to difficulties in employment and wage restructuring and make it hard to attract investors.) Workers in Chile got 5 to 10 percent of shares at a discount; a special financing scheme allowed them to borrow up to 50 percent of their severance pay to purchase shares, with a promise that the shares would be repurchased if they were worth less than their severance pay at the time of retirement. In Nigeria at least 10 percent of each SOE is reserved for employees; similar schemes exist in Argentina, Jamaica, Pakistan, Poland, and Venezuela, among others. Costs in lost revenue, usually low to begin with, are outweighed by the benefits of such schemes.

Avoid new investments. Some argue that the government will get a better price for SOEs that are physically rehabilitated before sale. But there are many reasons why large new investments for enterprises should be left to private owners once a decision has been made to privatize the enterprise. First, governments typically do not have a good record of making investment decisions and judging the market, and there is little evidence that they recover the costs of physical restructuring in the form of higher sales prices. Second, governments often lack the money to pay for investments in rehabilitation and modernization; getting the private sector to finance and manage such improvements— and take the risk—is a major reason for privatization in the first place. And third, governments have found that restructuring can delay privatization.

Box 12. *End-of-Service Benefits and Privatization in Ghana*

Most of Ghana's SOEs are overstaffed. Either the government must dismiss large numbers of employees before selling the SOEs, or it must allow new private owners to scale down the work force to an appropriate level.. A complicating factor is that the enterprises had previously agreed to over-generous severance pay and retirement benefits in collective bargaining agreements. Between 1985 and 1991 liabilities for these end-of-service benefits grew 150 percent, reaching between 0.5 million and 1 million cedis per employee ($1,423–$2,846), or four to seven times the country's GNP per capita. For the 150,000 employees in the state-owned sector, liabilities for unfunded retirement benefits alone were estimated at 75 billion cedis ($211 million) in December 1990. The government cannot afford these costly benefits, and few private investors would be interested in purchasing the SOEs if they had to honor these commitments.

Early in the privatization program, the government elected to pay off the end-of-service benefits from sale proceeds. Since proceeds were falling far short of liabilities, it arranged to supplement the benefits with annual budgetary contributions. Thus, with the help of a World Bank structural adjustment loan, Ghana's 1991 budget set aside 3.5 billion cedis for end-of-service benefits. These allocations have not been sufficient, and in the enterprises divested to date, the government has paid out only 20 percent of the benefits due employees.

The absence of a clear plan for settling these benefit liabilities has delayed the privatization of the large SOEs and has led to diminishing private sector interest. Roughly 22,000 redundant SOE employees remain on the government payroll, and some officials hope that the state can transfer the heavy burden of end-of-service benefits to private investors. Vested interests have seized on the benefits issue to stall the program. Breaking the logjam would require that the government renegotiate affordable settlements with the unions and spread payments over several years.

To avoid future trouble, the government has established a national pension scheme to replace the system of negotiating separate enterprise pension plans, and it is considering the creation of a national contributory unemployment scheme. It has also frozen the retirement gratuity portion of the end-of-service benefits at December 1990 levels and has called on SOE boards to renegotiate the benefits with their employees. As of December 1991 the government had also drafted a proposal to standardize retroactive end-of-service benefits.

Pricing and Valuation

Letting the market decide the sales price through competitive bidding procedures is critical for speed and transparency. At the same time, asset valuation can be essential for setting a benchmark for sales and ensuring a fair and above-board process.[29] In small and medium-size enterprises operating in competitive markets, little formal valuation might be required; Chile, the former German Democratic Republic, Mexico, and Tunisia more or less left asset valuation to the market in such cases. For large firms and monopolies a baseline valuation is more important. But even here, market-based pricing should be the preferred strategy provided there is (a) a careful prequalification of bidders on the basis of proposed business plans, the experience and qualifications of the operating company, and the extent to which the sale would concentrate market power to the detriment of consumers' interests, and (b) specification of a regulatory environment that provides incentives for modernization.

An overemphasis on valuation can prove problematic. Valuing SOEs for sale is not a science. Even in countries with sophisticated capital markets, technical appraisals seldom estimate correctly the market price of assets that have never been traded before. In developing countries SOE valuations are all the more tricky: the macroeconomic and operating environment is changing rapidly (the number of bids over the asking price for one of Mexico's airlines went from zero to seven after the government signed a debt renegotiation agreement); financial data are of poor quality and reliability (Argentine telecommunications had poor financial statements for the two years preceding sale); existing accounts do not conform to acceptable commercial standards (a problem that is most acute in Eastern Europe and Central Asia); comparables are few; and the market is thin.

Moreover, overvaluation and unrealistic expectations on the part of government create serious delays. Many divesting governments have chosen to set asking prices on the basis of historical book value—on the seemingly reasonable grounds that they wish to recover at least what they put in—but this has often led to valuations of eroded assets that bear little resemblance to what any buyer will offer. (In some cases, the result might be undervaluation, since book values are not adjusted for inflation.) In Costa Rica, for example, the ALUMASA aluminum mill was valued at $52 million on the basis of book value, despite persistent heavy losses. There were no takers at that price. The government then used a comparable mill in Venezuela, valued at about $8 million, as a reference price. ALUMASA was finally sold for $4 million, about 7.5 percent of book value.[30] In Puerto Rico the asking price for the telephone company was fixed in the legislation authorizing the sale, and the government had no room to maneuver during negotiations. The company was subsequently taken off the sale block after failing to obtain the floor price. And in Jamaica overvaluation delayed privatization, leading in the end to lower prices (20 percent of asking price in some cases) because of the physical and financial deterioration of assets during the protracted run-up to sale.

Overpricing shares in a public offering is another recipe for failure. In Sri Lanka, for example, 65 percent of the shares of United Motors remained with the underwriters, severely undermining small investors' confidence in public issues. In Turkey the share prices for two privatized enterprises have declined in value in relation to the stock exchange index by 50 and 38 percent, respectively, since their initial offerings in 1990. The shares appear to have been overpriced to begin with: investors have lost a total of 450 billion liras (in May 1991 prices) and have become wary about participating in future public offerings.[31] The lesson is that prices have to be low enough to foster demand, ensure a full subscription, and achieve the underlying objective of distributing ownership. Discounts on privatization sales have been much higher than the traditional after-market premium of 10 to 15 percent in other flotations (table 3). Gains to small investors might be viewed as a measure of success rather than as a financial loss to governments, since in such sales distributing ownership is more important than raising revenues. (As noted, if maximizing revenues is the goal, another method should be used.)

To offset potential political and financial costs, some countries offer discounts to small investors and ask higher prices, either fixed or by tender, from institutional investors.[32] Governments have also sold shares in tranches. France and the United Kingdom typically started with smaller share offerings and higher discounts; over time, as commitment was demonstrated and private sector confidence increased, larger percentages were offered, and discounts declined. Thus, the first half of British Aerospace was sold in 1981 for 150 million pounds; in 1985 the second half was sold for 275.3 million pounds. "Clawback clauses" allow government to share in the gains that an enterprise might make through subsequent sale of undervalued property. This mechanism was used in the sale of the twelve regional electricity distribution companies in the United Kingdom; the government was entitled to a proportion of any gain in the subsequent disposal of land and buildings.

Table 3. Prices for Selected Public Share Offers, 1979–87

Country	Enterprise	Date	Subscription price (local currency)	First day closing price (local currency)	Premium or discount (percent)
France	Compagnie Généréle d'Electricité	05/87	FF 290	FF 323	11.4
	Paribas	01/87	FF 405	FF 480	18.5
	Saint-Gobain	11/86	FF 310	FF 369	19.0
	Sogenal	03/87	FF 125	FF 225	80.0
Jamaica	National Commercial Bank	12/86	J$ 2.95	J$ 4.94	67.5
	Caribbean Cement Co.	06/87	J$ 2.00	J$ 1.55	– 22.5
Philippines	Philippine National Bank	n.a.	P 170	P 255	50.0
United Kingdom	British Airways	02/87	125 p	169 p	35.2
	British Gas	12/86	135 p	148 p	9.3
	British Petroleum	11/79	363 p	367 p	1.1
	British Telecom	12/84	130 p	173 p	33.1
	Rolls Royce	05/87	170 p	232 p	36.5

Source: For France, Durupty 1991; for Jamaica, Leeds 1987a; for Philippines, World Bank, Country Economics Department; for United Kingdom, Vickers and Yarrow 1988.

Financing

Overcoming Financing Constraints

In many developing countries financing constraints stem from weak financial systems. In Ghana, for instance, the five major banks had a total of $2.1 million for acquisition financing, while the estimated value of the SOEs up for sale in the first round exceeded $25 million—more than the total net worth of the banks. Government decisions further worsen these constraints. A number of governments (for example, in Argentina, Jamaica, and the Philippines) have put SOEs on the market while simultaneously offering high-yield, low-risk, tax-free government bonds. In these cases, poor timing of sales dampened the market for some SOE shares.

Sensitivity about foreign ownership exists in all countries, developing and industrial. For political and social reasons, governments are generally reluctant to cede to foreign investors control over assets, especially those they consider of strategic importance, and have therefore restricted external participation in privatization. Such restrictions have narrowed the range of financing options, particularly in the sale of large SOEs. Restrictions on foreign ownership exclude countries from an important source of new capital, markets, management, and technology. Prior restrictions on foreign involvement in many countries formerly averse to the concept, such as India and Mexico, have consequently been eased; in country after country the rules are being relaxed, and competition to obtain foreign investment is growing intense. With foreign as well as domestic investors, success largely depends on having a stable economic and regulatory environment in place, as is illustrated by the examples of Chile and Mexico. In nontradable sectors, in particular, guarantees regarding convertibility and profit repatriation will be necessary to attract foreign investors.

Political concerns can be reduced in a manner consistent with social and political objectives by reserving a "golden share" for government (but only under exceptional circumstances—in very large SOEs serving the national interest, for example) or by combining sale of a controlling interest to a foreign investor with widespread distribution of the remaining shares to citizens and employees.[33] In Indonesia, New Zealand, and Togo SOEs have been sold to foreigners with the stipulation that a certain amount of shares be gradually floated to small investors through the stock market.

Foreign direct investment has been increasing since the mid-1980s. Nonetheless, in a sample of forty developing countries it accounts for only 10 percent of all private investment (Pfeffermann and Madarassy 1992). This implies that the bulk of SOEs will have to be sold to domestic investors. Yet governments have often curtailed the domestic market by excluding certain ethnic groups from participating in privatization or by favoring certain groups, for political reasons. In East and South Asia commercially oriented and relatively wealthy minority groups are discriminated against in the privatization process. In East Africa citizens of Asian origin are sometimes excluded; in Kenya, where privatization has been debated since the early 1980s, few sales have taken place, primarily because of the sensitive political nature of the division of national assets between African citizens and those of Asian origin (the likely buyers of SOEs in any unrestricted sale). Such restrictions and concessions can lead to costly delays and limit the entry of groups that possess the necessary capital, skills, and experience to provide jobs and opportunities for the majority. Mechanisms such as the reservation or subsequent dilution of a portion of shares for certain groups need to be developed to mitigate political concerns and safeguard the interests of the majority while at the same time tapping the expertise and resources of the minorities.

Government attempts to curb the participation of institutional investors and financial institutions also make it hard to finance privatization.
Regulation of weak financial systems is clearly a legitimate function of
government, but this should not preclude institutional investors from
playing a positive catalytic role in privatization. In turn, privatization
can help to strengthen and diversify financial markets. After Chile
addressed the problems created by poor banking practices during its
first sales, it was naturally reluctant to allow banks or even private
pension funds to invest in SOE shares. It solved the problem by creating
a special commission to classify the risk of these investments—very
conservatively—and by limiting the amount of high-risk shares pension
funds can hold.

Financial intermediaries should not be forced to buy, however. To
soak up excess liquidity and provide equity to SOEs, Brazil compelled
financial institutions and pension funds to convert a portion of their
assets to "privatization certificates" for the purchase of SOE shares. Not
surprisingly, the financial institutions initially opposed this idea. Brazilian
insurance companies and pension funds argued that they could not
invest in privatized firms because their regulations prevented them from
investing in high-risk ventures (although they have participated in some
recent large privatizations—in steel and petrochemicals, for example).
Banks have reportedly purchased only a small portion of the shares they
were expected to buy in the preliminary auctions. Forced acquisition
schemes run counter to the fiduciary obligations and sound business
practices of these intermediaries and do nothing to improve management. Indeed, financial discipline could be weakened by placing new
funds in the hands of managers who have done nothing to raise the
funds.

Debt versus Cash

There are excellent reasons to sell for cash, even if this means selling at
a lower price. Outright sale cleanly severs the ownership link between
enterprise and state; "cutting the umbilical cord" was an important
consideration in Mexico and Venezuela. The Mexican government insisted on all cash sales to ensure that unpaid balances could not be used
by the new owners to "blackmail" the state for future concessions. Cash
sales also provide the liquidity to pay enterprise liabilities and severance
benefits. They should be regarded as the preferred payment method.

Nevertheless, many developing countries have no alternative but to
sell for debt, usually financed by the seller (the government). Easing the
constraints on participation by foreigners and institutional investors will

help, but many SOEs are simply not sufficiently attractive and many financial systems not deep enough to attract equity or bank financing. Selling on the "installment plan" is one option, but settling for a lower sale price, selling in tranches (with control passing to the private sector), or simply giving small assets away might be better solutions than excessive use of debt to ease financing constraints.

Highly leveraged sales, regardless of whether the seller (the government) or the banks are the source of credit, are risky. In Chile the failure of privatized firms between 1974 and 1984 was partly due to the large debts owed to the government. The initial terms were attractive: buyers were to pay 10 to 20 percent down, with one year's grace. After that, however, they faced a short (five to seven years) repayment period, at a real interest rate of 8 to 12 percent. The firms had a very thin equity cushion when the recession hit in the early 1980s; seven of every ten privatized companies went into bankruptcy and reverted back to state hands when their controlling banks were nationalized. In the second round of sales the chastened government gave no credit (except to the smallest investors and employees), and bidders had to prove their solvency. Numerous other examples of the problems involved in granting and recovering debt could be cited.

Debt-Equity Swaps

Swaps can ease financing constraints and help improve a country's investment climate (Sung 1991). But care is needed to ensure that the deal is to the country's benefit. In a debt-equity swap the debt holder who wants to buy the enterprise swaps debt worth a fraction of its face value in the secondary market for equity, usually at a rate that is better than the secondary market price but still well below the face value. In Argentina, as noted, swaps in privatizations reduced the face value of outstanding commercial bank debt by 20 percent.

Swaps may be a way for heavily indebted countries to bring foreign investors, including commercial banks, into transactions that might not go through without their participation. A substantial proportion of the swaps under privatization are believed to have involved the original commercial bank lenders. A case in point is the Argentine telecommunications deal. The government sought a buyer who would bring in an experienced operating company, invest $5 billion in capital improvements over ten years, and maximize debt reduction. (Companies' bids were expressed in terms of external debt.) Argentina sold the company in November 1990 for $214 million in cash and a $2 billion reduction in the face value of its debt. The advisers on this deal believe that it would never

have materialized—particularly with a pledge for new investment—
without the swap to induce participation by commercial banks. The
approach used was to price the swaps through an auction; this allowed
the government to capture a larger share of the discount than under
case-by-case negotiation (as in Chile; see box 13).

Nevertheless, swaps must be used carefully. Critics of swaps argue
with some justification that the government may be better off selling the
enterprise and using the proceeds of the sale to repay or repurchase the
debt on the secondary market. It might in that way capture more of the
discount and expand the participation of local investors. Mexico, for
example, sold most of its SOEs without swaps and is using the proceeds
to buy back debt. But Mexico's debt reduction under the Brady plan put
it in a better position to attract investors than many other heavily
indebted countries. Other debtor countries may have less choice, as a
large debt overhang may deter investors from buying SOEs, especially if
they are large companies that require new investments. In these circumstances, debt-equity swaps can be useful.[34]

Countries may be able to increase their access to swaps by creating
conversion funds for privatization. These funds, which have been successfully used in Argentina, Chile, and the Philippines, pool eligible debt
paper from commercial banks, multinational investors, and individual
investors to swap for enterprise assets. Such funds could even be active
investors, taking a role in restructuring poorly managed enterprises.

Financing Postprivatization Investments

In many of the Bank's borrower countries the domestic private sector
lacks access to capital for modernizing and expanding privatized firms.
And even where foreign investors are welcome, their calculations of
noncommercial risk may lead them to reject financially attractive opportunities to purchase SOEs. This is particularly likely in privatizations of
infrastructure and other nontradables where, because sales revenues are
in local currency, buyers will be especially concerned about exchange
risk and convertibility. In many developing countries the process of
obtaining financing for postprivatization investment may thus require
external assistance and support.

Recent evidence from Latin America shows that in countries with
sound macroeconomic and regulatory frameworks, investment capital
can usually be raised without external assistance. But where perceptions
of country risk are high, some assistance from international agencies and
bilateral donors in accessing financial markets may be required to ensure
availability of private funds for expanding investments in newly privat-

Box 13. Debt-Equity Swaps in Chile

Chile's debt swap program, in effect between 1985 and 1991, is considered one of the most successful in the world. Its aims were to use the discounts available on Chile's international commercial bank debt to reduce external debt, attract foreign participation, and repatriate Chilean capital held abroad. Several factors contributed to the success of the program. Clear-cut swap rules are contained in Chapters XVIII and XIX of Chile's Compendium of Rules on International Exchange. Chapter XVIII allows the conversion of foreign debt into a peso obligation and is aimed at Chilean investors who may have access to capital abroad. Chapter XIX is designed to accommodate equity investment by foreigners via debt cancellation. Whereas similar conversion programs in other countries have been suspended or drastically modified from time to time, the Chilean program remained stable over the years. This consistency was important in inducing potential investors to make additional investments through debt swaps.

The definition of eligible debt under the program is broad and includes all commercial bank debt except short-term maturities. Swap proceeds may be used for broad investment activities or for refinancing local currency debt. Since use of Chapter XIX requires prior authorization of projects, the Central Bank was able to ration approvals to control the effects of swaps on inflation and exchange rates. Stringent limits were enforced on repatriation of profits and capital derived from the investment made. Careful design and implementation of the program reduced round-tripping, under which investors would have been encouraged to take funds abroad and bring them back through swaps. The effective implementation of the program by the authorities, as well as the supportive macroeconomic environment and active privatization programs of Chile since the mid-1980s, helped build confidence in the system among potential investors and make the swap program a success.

During the six years that the Chilean program was in operation, the two swap schemes retired about $7 billion in commercial bank debt, representing about 30 percent of the total. About 20 percent of Chapter XIX swap deals involved investments in privatized public enterprises in various economic sectors such as agribusiness, manufacturing, and banks and other financial institutions. The pace of conversion under Chapter XIX fell off sharply in 1991 as the secondary market price of eligible debt rose to 90 percent of the face value and discounts on the declining debt stock became extremely limited.

ized enterprises. Such support is currently provided to private investors by the IFC and, more recently, through MIGA. Moreover, the World Bank Group has contributed and will continue to contribute to the creation of an enabling environment for private sector development; indeed, a major role of the Bank is to assist its borrowers to reach the stage at which no guarantees of any sort are necessary.

Managing Privatization

Privatization requires a managerial setup that ensures speed, transparency, and consistency in implementation. Improvised arrangements can derail the whole process. In the early phase of privatization in Togo, for example, speedy decisionmaking was hampered by lack of clarity about the roles and responsibilities of the various ministries. And in Turkey the lack of procedures for public accountability and the weak design of the institutional setup led to delays in the early part of the program.

The Importance of Transparency

One of the principal lessons of experience is that every privatization transaction must be transparent. Transparency can be ensured through clear and simple selection criteria for evaluating bids, clearly defined competitive bidding procedures, disclosure of purchase price and buyer, well-defined institutional responsibilities, and adequate monitoring and supervision of the program. Lack of transparency can lead to a political backlash and is often associated with poorly structured—and very costly—sales. In Guinea SOEs were closed and sales were negotiated without proper legal authorization; many potentially beneficial sales were subsequently halted. The government is now considering the establishment of a review agency to protect the interests of the state, increase transparency, and expedite the process. In Mexico, where sector ministries conducted initial sales without clear guidelines for bidding and evaluation, the ensuing public outcry over apparently poor deals led to the creation of a central supervising institution for privatization, with clear guidelines and procedures (see below). And in Pakistan lack of due diligence and attention to transparency is leading to slow execution (and to some court cases involving contested sales), despite strong political resolve for rapid privatization.

Lack of transparency can lead to a perception—justified or not—of unfair dealing and to a popular outcry that can threaten not only privatization but also reform in general. Yet excessive devotion to transparency need not become an excuse for inaction. For industrial and commercial firms operating in competitive or potentially competitive markets, all that is normally needed is light management and review of transactions; Mexico and the former German Democratic Republic, for example, divested hundreds of enterprises in this way. Microenterprises can be divested even more rapidly, as the experience of Czechoslovakia, the former German Democratic Republic, and Poland shows. Competitive bidding ensures both transparency and speed. In these instances the assets should be put to productive use speedily to reduce the administrative burden on the state and avoid opportunities for vested interests to coalesce.

The larger and more visible the transaction, and the less competitive the market for the enterprise's goods or services, the greater the importance of transparency. To avoid delays, many countries have established special commissions outside the regular privatization machinery to handle the sale of large firms that operate as monopolies (as in the sale of telephone companies in Jamaica, Mexico, and Venezuela). Foreign advisers have also been hired as a way of keeping the process both transparent and speedy.

Centralizing Policy Responsibilities

Transparency and speed are best achieved by centralizing policy responsibilities for privatization in a strong focal point. A clear mandate, sufficient autonomy, minimal bureaucracy, ready access to top decisionmakers, and quality staff are conditions for success. In the second and principal phase of privatization in Mexico, for example, a unit of seven people in the Ministry of Finance, reporting directly to an interministerial commission of key ministers-and freed of public sector rules and regulations, divested hundreds of enterprises over a few years. In the Philippines the Asset Privatization Trust, headed by a qualified private sector businessman and staffed by a small group of experienced private sector individuals paid at private sector rates, disposed of more than 150 nonperforming assets in two years. By contrast, in Ghana and Jamaica the process became lengthy and bureaucratic, the supervisory agency lacked clout and authority over sector ministries, and recruitment of key staff was delayed because of noncompetitive salaries.

Cabinet commissions and sector ministries do not function well as focal points. They tend to delay privatization because of strong vested interests and to make the process less transparent. For example, early privatization efforts in Brazil stalled because sector ministries were slow to privatize; implementation is expected to pick up speed following the creation of the Privatization Commission and its secretariat.

Decentralizing Implementation

Although decisionmaking is best centralized, implementation should be decentralized to accelerate the process and reduce the workload of the central unit. Responsibility for implementation can be delegated to banks and financial institutions (as in France, Mexico, and Nigeria), to international and local business consultancies (Argentina and Venezuela), to holding companies (the Philippines), and to SOE managers themselves (Czechoslovakia, Hungary, Tunisia, and Turkey). The privatization authority must supervise these implementing agencies and have a clear mandate and timetable for privatization; otherwise, the risk of inaction is great. In Tunisia SOE managers, closely monitored by the Privatization Commission, moved quickly because they recognized that their careers were at stake. Clear implementation principles and standards of accountability are also necessary to minimize abuse and ensure transparency.

Employing the Right Skills for Privatization

Government capacity to handle the privatization process is scarce; time and money have to be spent obtaining the right technical, financial, and legal skills. Small privatizations can and should be handled locally to the extent possible (as in Mexico), but skills may need to be imported in low-income countries (where institutional weakness has been a major contributor to privatization delays) and for large transactions. Government capacity to employ external advice and assess the public policy implications of the advice needs to be strengthened almost everywhere, particularly since the short time horizons and success-based fee structures of investment bankers can create perverse incentives.

5. Privatization in Eastern Europe and Central Asia

Even at their peak, the largest SOE sectors in industrial and mixed economies were small in comparison with those in socialist Eastern Europe and Central Asia. At the beginning of the 1990s enterprise numbers in this region were much larger than anywhere else, and SOEs accounted for between two-thirds and nine-tenths of all productive economic activity.[35] Indeed, SOEs were not and are not a "sector"; they constitute, in effect, the bulk of the nonagricultural economy.

Past Performance

In the past, impressive production figures were reported for SOEs in most command economies. Methods of production, however, were inefficient, and the goods produced were generally poor in quality and incapable of competing in export markets. Despite persistent partial reform efforts from the 1960s onward, the SOEs never achieved the efficiency and productivity expected of them, and their performance deteriorated sharply in the period 1970–89. Dissatisfaction with the meager results of past partial reforms and the contribution of inefficient SOEs to stagnating or even declining standards of living contributed to the political-economic upheaval of the past several years and to a widespread enthusiasm for privatization. All the successor governments in the region have already launched or are planning privatizations.

The Turn toward Privatization

Privatization in the former socialist countries differs greatly from that elsewhere. First, it is a more massive and thus a more complex undertaking. For example, the governments of Czechoslovakia, Hungary, Poland, and Romania have announced intentions to privatize between a third and a half of their SOEs within a three-year period. At a conservative estimate, this amounts to more than 8,000 firms (and probably many more, as conglomerates and oversized units are broken into manageable, salable units). In the past eighteen months the former German Democratic Republic alone has privatized more enterprises than the rest of the world has in the past fifteen years.

Second, the context is very different. In even the poorest or least market-oriented developing country there is a private sector of sorts, some prices bear a relation to scarcity values, and concepts of property, ownership, title, and contract are acknowledged (if not always rigorously or regularly enforced). This has not been the case in the former socialist countries for at least forty years—longer, for the former U.S.S.R.

Third, the goals are different; that is, they are more overtly sociopolitical than elsewhere. In mixed economies privatization is seen primarily as a tool for enhancing efficiency and reducing budgetary burdens, not as an end in itself. In contrast, in the former socialist economies there is a strong argument that privatization is an end in itself because it is the principal mechanism for moving society from communism to capitalism. Its overriding purpose is to transfer property rights to owners who have incentives for defending the interests of the capital they own. Private owners are expected to support with their votes and their actions the painful steps necessary for transiting fully to a market economy. For the transition to succeed, privatization must be massive, since it must create a property-owning group of sufficient size to carry economic and political weight. In sum, the purpose of privatization is to transform society, as well as to put previously wasted and underutilized assets to more productive use.

There is near-universal agreement in these countries on the goal of creating a large and influential group of property owners. Some go further and insist that the property transfer must be accomplished immediately, since many key decisions that will determine the nature of the postcommunist system are being made now. The fear is that if privatization does not come quickly, it will take years for any substantial portion of assets to pass into private hands. And in the interim, a base could be constituted for those who see interventionist populism as the less-painful alternative to free-market economics.

Other respected reformers argue that since "the prime purpose of privatization is to nurture the incentive force private ownership provides," each transaction should be structured to yield the maximum possible amount of macroeconomic and microeconomic gain and "the sale of state property should not be governed by the guiding principle of speed" (Kornai 1990, p. 93). This view is more common in countries that had a more evolutionary than revolutionary break with communism; in these circumstances leaders are less likely to regard massive and rapid privatization as essential. For example, in Hungary, where the break with the communist past was spread over a number of years, management buyouts are the main privatization method. In Czechoslovakia, in contrast, the great majority of firms are to be privatized by a "voucher" or giveaway method that emphasizes speed and aims at the rapid elimination of government involvement in the enterprise sector.

Obstacles to Privatization and Ways around Them

The pressures to privatize are intense. At the time of writing, more than 800 medium-size and large enterprises in the region (excluding the former German Democratic Republic) have become private. The number is at the same time large and disappointing: large both absolutely and in comparison with achievements elsewhere, disappointing in comparison with what these governments were hoping to accomplish. This relatively slow pace is attributable to conditions that make the normally complex privatization process doubly difficult in former socialist countries.

- The legal basis for private ownership is unclear or embryonic and the claimants to property rights are numerous and competing.
- The elaborate auditing, consulting, and financial apparatus for preparing a firm for sale must be built from scratch or imported at high cost.
- The domestic population is illiquid, capital markets are virtually nonexistent, the banking and credit system is in desperate shape, and the only likely domestic buyers are members of the usually distrusted and discredited *nomenklatura*.
- The vested interests arrayed against privatization are powerful. Moreover, newly elected governments, struggling with democracy, fear that privatization—and the liberalizations of prices, the trade regime, and interest and wage rates that normally accompany privatization—may bring about the collapse of much of the industrial base, skyrocketing unemployment, inequities in the distribution of property, and grievous sociopolitical disruption.

These obstacles are real and formidable. Unemployment has risen from, in effect, zero to more than 11 percent of the work force in Poland in the past two years, and reforms in other countries seem destined to produce similar figures. The collapse of the Council of Mutual Economic Assistance (CMEA) trade bloc has exacerbated, but does not fully account for, the dramatic declines in industrial production in the region. Nascent democracies find it difficult to enforce painful reforms and win votes at the same time.

Nonetheless, governments in the former socialist countries, with external assistance, are devising innovative methods for overcoming the serious obstacles that face privatization.

- If enterprises cannot be sold easily or quickly, perhaps they can be given away, as is proposed or under way in Czechoslovakia, Poland, Romania, and several republics of the former U.S.S.R.
- If buyers are illiquid, owner-assisted financing can be arranged, as in Hungary.
- Workers who fear and oppose privatization can be provided with a "sweetener" in the form of free or low-cost shares in the newly privatized firms, as in Hungary, Poland, Russia and parts of Yugoslavia.
- Where citizens do not (and cannot in the present economic circumstances) have adequate information about which enterprises to invest in, mutual funds or holding companies can be established to bundle firms and diversify risk, as is being done in Czechoslovakia, Poland, and Romania and as is proposed in Russia.
- Where citizens fear that members of the *nomenklatura* are making off with the assets at unfair prices, reviewing agencies can regulate the process in the public interest, as in Hungary, Poland, and Russia.
- Where excessive centralization of the process is causing delays, decentralized implementation with overall central monitoring and control can be attempted, as in Hungary and Russia.
- Where overstaffing needs to be addressed, social safety nets and unemployment insurance schemes must be devised.

Implementation of these mechanisms is only just beginning, and in some instances, using them to solve one problem may cause another. For example, Poland and Romania have had problems setting up the proposed investment intermediaries. Giving away enterprises can be almost as difficult as selling them, especially if the goal is to turn them around as well. Czechoslovakia has experienced difficulties in processing the masses of information necessary to launch the voucher scheme, causing delay in the start date. Striking a balance between supervision and strangulation is not easy; the reviewing agencies set up to regulate privatization have sometimes brought it to a halt. Elsewhere in the world, governments that have given credit to enterprise purchasers have often found that repayment is a problem and that purchasers with little of their own capital at risk are less than perfect owners. This is likely to happen in the former socialist countries as well. Giving shares to workers could lead to excessive wage bills, impede further and needed reform, and scare off other investors or lenders. Finally, unemployment insurance schemes can be brought into existence fairly quickly, but improving the availability of other factors that contribute to increased labor mobility, such as housing, is a longer-term effort.

In sum, in the former socialist countries, even more than elsewhere, not all the answers on what methods will and will not work are available, and there is uncertainty concerning what will be the by-products of the corrective or facilitative mechanisms listed above. Arguing for further delays, however, would be exactly the wrong advice, since delays might weaken or even derail the entire transformation process. The costs of inaction and delay are great. Presently, thousands of enterprises receive neither central commands nor adequate market signals; this lack of direction is the worst possible situation. The World Bank's emphasis in supporting privatization in these countries should not be on avoiding risk but on ensuring flexibility.

Mass Privatization

Mass privatization in the former socialist countries could take several forms: simply turning over ownership to the current managers and workers; making all or some enterprises into joint stock companies and distributing a percentage of shares to the current managers and workers; creating mutual funds-cum-holding companies and distributing shares to the public; distributing to the public vouchers or coupons that entitle them to bid directly on shares in individual firms; and several variations in between. All these methods are under consideration or in process in the former socialist countries. This book cannot report on them, since none has yet gotten off the ground. The Polish scheme, which is scheduled to come into effect in 1992, will assign groups of large enterprises— 200 or more at first—to between five and twenty financial intermediary institutions, the shares of which will be given to the Polish people at low or no cost. The more ambitious "coupon privatization" scheme in Czechoslovakia aims to transfer 3,000 large and medium-size firms to private hands by the end of 1992 by giving citizens the chance to exchange their assignment of low-cost vouchers for shares in individual companies or in investment funds. The Romanian government intends to create five public ownership funds that will hold minority shares in all commercial companies and whose shares will be distributed free to the Romanian public. The government of Russia proposes to give workers 25 percent of the shares of all enterprises turned into joint stock companies and the option to purchase another 10 percent at a discount.

There are several advantages to the mass approaches. They avoid problems of absorptive capacity and purchasing power by rapidly giving at least some ownership in a firm or firms to a population that cannot—or would not—purchase it. They are equitable, since under the proposed schemes all or most of the population receives shares at no cost or is given the chance to obtain shares at low cost—although one could argue against the Russian proposal on the grounds that only those working in viable firms receive shares of any value. Mass privatization would delay, if not entirely prevent, the accumulation of property by the *nomenklatura*. (This could be a disadvantage if the *nomenklatura* has the best managerial potential.) Mass schemes may also reduce the need for government-funded or -administered restructuring and allow governments to focus funding on priority tasks such as developing social safety nets and investing in infrastructure.

But there are also risks. Mass privatization is an untested approach; there is but the slightest evidence (from the recent and unanalyzed Mongolian experience) on how these schemes will actually work. Mass privatization is an institutionally complex process that requires good administration by admittedly weak and overburdened governments. Most important, widely dispersed ownership without a core investor-manager does not solve the problem of corporate governance; it does not put "a living, breathing entrepreneur" in charge of the assets (Kornai 1990). The forms of mass privatization that transfer large percentages of shares to workers may slow full privatization, deter large commitments by private investors, foreign or domestic, or cause future difficulties for a lead or majority investor.

In sum, the uncertain situation in the former socialist countries calls for flexibility; mistakes are bound to occur. Governments and the World Bank should actively support a variety of approaches, including experimental ones such as mass privatization (as indeed the Bank has done in Romania and Poland). As experience accumulates, those that work best should be strengthened and mistakes or oversights corrected. But although the optimal set of tactics for the former socialist economies may not yet be clear, the general strategy for achieving their objectives, given the special country circumstances, is apparent: these countries should privatize, they should privatize in all ways possible that encourage competition, and they should adopt methods that do far more than privatize firms one-by-one, including the transformation of all enterprises into joint stock companies.

Notes

1. The World Bank Group comprises the International Bank for Reconstruction and Development (IBRD) and its affiliates, the International Finance Corporation (IFC), the International Development Association (IDA), and the Multilateral Investment Guarantee Agency (MIGA).

2. All dollar amounts are current U.S. dollars, unless otherwise specified. A billion is a thousand million.

3. Domestic welfare is measured by changes in costs and benefits for all the economic actors affected by the privatization—that is, buyers, governments, consumers, workers, and competitors.

4. Privatization is sometimes more broadly defined to include deregulation and new private sector entry, or private sector financing through build-operate-transfer (BOT) arrangements. The book does not examine these broader mechanisms, which raise a different and complex set of issues; it concentrates on lessons derived from ownership transfer.

5. It could be argued that these losses do not matter if the money spent laid the base, through investments or training, for future profitable activity. The problem is that in too many cases investments in SOEs have not produced a cost-covering stream of income; promises regarding improved performance have often not been fulfilled.

6. See Nellis (1989a). Performance contracts aim to clarify SOE goals and establish a clear set of targets between government and enterprise. They have been widely used in Sub-Saharan Africa. Although they have proved somewhat useful in establishing a dialogue between owner and enterprise, they have been generally ineffective in enforcing financial commitments between the government and the SOE. An exception may be the Gambian case in which, reportedly, strict enforcement by the government of the conditions imposed in several performance agreements led to management changes and, subsequently, to improved performance in three firms to which the device was applied.

7. See Shirley (1989a). The performance evaluation system holds management accountable for achieving agreed objectives that have been calculated as annual targets. Performance indicators were tailored to each SOE and included, among other things, general indicators relating operating expenses to sales, delivery of goods or services, control of administrative expenses, management of funds, and research and development.

8. These numbers would be much higher if the very large number of completed "small" privatizations of shops, microenterprises, and kiosks in the retail and services sectors were included. An estimated 80,000 such firms have been privatized in Poland, 7,000 in Czechoslovakia, 1,100 in Hungary, and 13,000 in the former German Democratic Republic. Other former socialist countries, including Russia, have announced ambitious "small" privatization programs that will be launched in 1992.

9. In contrast to earlier partial studies, the Bank study addresses the effects of divestiture on all important actors. In assessing the long-run impact of divestiture, it also overcomes two methodological shortcomings of many earlier analyses by (a) isolating the effect that privatization has on firm behavior from concurrent changes (for instance,

changes in macroeconomic policy, technology, demand structure, or the regulatory framework) and (b) answering the counterfactual question, what would have happened to performance in the absence of ownership change? This exercise required laborious extrapolation of preprivatization performance trends, combined with measures to take exogenous changes into account.

10. An argument can be made that governments could have relaxed the investment constraint without selling SOEs. But most developing country governments face a hard budget constraint, any deviations from which can lead to adverse macroeconomic effects, decrease country creditworthiness, or both. Moreover, making large investments in productive SOEs diverts scarce resources away from priority tasks.

11. After divestiture, and as a result of the adoption of the RPI-X regulatory formula, prices changed more regularly than before. Prior to privatization, British Telecom had no rate-of-return bands that would have automatically triggered price increases. Price changes were made only when achieved rates of return were substantially out of line with the target rates. Also, prices of service elements for which demand elasticity is low have been raised in relation to those for which the demand elasticity is higher, which probably would not have occurred under public ownership.

12. In most developing countries SOE employees at lower skill levels are more highly paid than their private sector counterparts, but SOE managers are less well remunerated than private sector managers. In Thailand, for example, SOE pay at the lower-skill level is almost double that of private enterprises; pay for middle-level professionals is 30–34 percent higher. Top executives, by contrast, are underpaid in comparison with their counterparts in the private sector.

13. Mexico's minister of finance has noted that the $10 billion losses of the state-owned steel complex (SIDERMEX) could have brought potable water, sewerage, hospitals, and education to many of the poor in southeastern Mexico. Much of SIDERMEX has now been privatized, and the funds formerly used to keep it alive are now available for tasks with a wider social impact.

14. Only a handful of cases have been researched carefully; data for many large developing country privatizations are not available.

15. Galal, Jones, Tandon, and Vogelsang (forthcoming). The study counted as consumers those who had not been paying for electricity; that they now had to pay was considered a consumer loss. This balanced the gains of payers, and the study concluded that consumers were unaffected by the sale. If one were to consider as legitimate consumers only those who previously had been paying, the case would have recorded substantial increases in consumer welfare.

16. Privatization "master plans" appeal to governments of an intervening bent, but the complexities and uncertainties of a major transaction—much less a set of transactions—strongly suggest that the divestiture process cannot be planned in intricate detail. What is required are straightforward policy directives or guidelines. Overplanning ended up delaying rather than promoting privatization in, for example, Malaysia and Turkey.

17. In this book a potentially competitive market is defined as one in which relaxation of legal or regulatory barriers to entry would reasonably be expected to produce, in the short- to medium-term, either domestic or foreign competitors.

18. In Chile tariffs are structured so that large consumers with high demand at peak periods, who cause the system to expand, pay a higher price than consumers who do not cause the system to expand; the latter group pays a price equivalent to the short-run marginal cost. Suppliers to large consumers have to compete in this segment of the market (see Galal, Jones, Tandon, and Vogelsang forthcoming).

19. Under private management the steel mill became profitable for the first time since its creation and diversified into a new product line, pylon manufacturing, which was more

labor-intensive than making reinforcing bars, its main product. Taxes paid increased, some jobs were preserved at higher salaries, and the political embarrassment of liquidation was avoided. Some think that the operation opened the door to subsequent privatization, which in the mid-1980s was significant in Togo. The inference is that even if the original deal was uneconomic, the net economic effect of private entry into the market might have been positive. This assertion has never been rigorously examined, but it is hard to believe that these secondary and intangible elements made up for the fact that the firm sold its prime product at 165,000 CFA francs a unit when the FOB price of imported reinforcing bars was 110,000 CFA francs a unit.

20. Experience shows that share ownership tends to concentrate over time, despite the mechanisms used to attract and retain small shareholders (such as bonuses or matching shares, pricing discounts, and reduced taxes on dividends). In the United Kingdom, although concerted efforts were made to spread shares widely in the privatization flotations, reconcentration of ownership occurred quickly. Similarly, at the time of the public issue of the Malaysian International Shipping Corporation, there were approximately 60,000 shareholders; the number fell to fewer than 5,000 after a brief round of secondary trading. Similar patterns emerge in other countries divesting through their stock markets (see Adam and Cavendish 1990). This appears to be true even in the former socialist countries. A 1992 case study on Russia notes that a worker-management buyout in 1991 resulted in an initial capital structure of 50 percent workers, 30 percent management, and 20 percent others; one year later management controlled more than 50 percent, while worker shareholding had fallen to about 30 percent as some workers took the opportunity for a quick cash profit.

21. The Mexicans see this as lesson number one of their successful experience. They recommend starting with small firms to learn how to do it, to educate the public, and to minimize risks. According to Pedro Aspe, Mexico's secretary of finance and public credit, "If one makes a mistake selling a night club or a bicycle factory . . . it is not as tragic as if these mistakes are made while selling the largest commercial bank in the country, the telephone company or a major airline" (Aspe 1991).

22. Ways of holding management accountable include business plans, properly staffed and empowered boards of directors, contract plans and performance agreements, and performance evaluation and incentive systems. All are costly and difficult to install; none is a foolproof method for improving performance.

23. A World Bank study of the NTT in cooperation with NTT International Corporation contains a great deal of useful information on how to prepare for privatization (see Takano 1992).

24. See Guislain (1992) for a detailed discussion of the different types of legal restructuring involved prior to privatization.

25. Debt relief should take place only when management changes hands and not before; otherwise there is a real risk that arrears will simply recur. In addition, other measures, such as improvements in collection of outstanding accounts receivable, freezing of nonessential capital expenditure, and reduction of inventory, should also be taken to avoid recurrence of arrears.

26. Many SOEs are severely overstaffed in comparison with estimates of the personnel needed to complete the assigned tasks and with private sector or industry norms. The extent of past overstaffing can be alarming. One regional railway in a borrower country had 4,500 employees prior to sale. A consulting firm estimated that the company could operate well with 2,900 employees (a one-third reduction). The new private owners, after a few months' operation, now estimate that they can comfortably run the company with 700 to 1,000 employees and still have more employees per freight-kilometer than many railways in the world.

27. Galenson (1989) and Svejnar and Terrell (1991) showed that the payback period for severance pay ranges from four months to seven years and that savings outweigh costs in a relatively short time, usually one to three years. Whether these clear financial gains indicate economic gains as well depends on the extent to which the released labor takes up more productive pursuits and on the uses to which the saved funds are put. Svejnar and Terrell's argument is that the savings are highly likely to be productively applied, since in all cases studied the marginal productivity of dismissed labor was zero or negative.

28. It has been argued that in Chile workers' shares also helped raise the price paid for SOEs because the buyers perceived that the workers' stake reduced the risks of renationalization (see Luders 1990).

29. Any company, private or public, can be valued on the basis of net asset value, net present value of discounted cash flow, earnings trends (price-earnings ratios), dividend yields, or a combination of these methods. Asset valuation is generally used for small loss-making enterprises that are to be sold on a piecemeal basis rather than as ongoing concerns. The discounted cash flow method, which calculates the present value of the projected stream of future cash earnings, is used when SOEs are sold as ongoing concerns. Price-earnings ratios (whereby the share price is calculated as a multiple of the company's earnings) and dividend yields are used to price SOE shares for sale through a public offering. Since there is no one correct value, more than one method is usually used to derive a range of values.

30. Many find shocking sales prices that are less than 10 percent of book value. They conclude that privatizations at such prices constitute a serious loss to, if not a crime by, the state. But the critics should also direct their ire at the people who built uneconomic enterprises or ran them so badly. The rational economic solution for firms that persistently run losses or are in a state of negative net worth is to accept any positive price offered, to give the firms away, or even to induce someone to take them over. Economically, it makes sense for owners to pay someone to take a liability-ridden entity off their hands and—it is hoped—put the assets back to productive use. The *Treuhand* has sold dozens of firms at the symbolic price of one mark. In these cases, according to *Treuhand* officials, "we are not selling companies; we are buying management and technology."

31. In the end, the Turkish government repurchased the shares to maintain the price and then resold them at later dates in smaller tranches. This was costly and set a bad precedent for the remaining public offerings.

32. Tender methods are more appropriate for sales of shares to well-informed financial institutions and trade buyers than to small investors; the former are better able to assess bid strategy and price the investment opportunity. Tenders were extensively applied in the public offerings in the United Kingdom.

33. The term "golden share" comes from the British privatization experience and refers to a stipulation, in a general privatization law or in a particular sales agreement, that government retain one nonvoting special share which gives it the power to reject the subsequent sale or a major capital or physical restructuring of the firm. New Zealand used a similar arrangement in some of its privatizations, with government retaining a "Kiwi share."

34. Paradoxically, the more successful are debt-equity swaps, the more their usefulness declines. As a country buys its debt back, it becomes a better credit risk; the secondary market discount on the debt drops, and this reduces the incentive for the investor. (This was one reason why the volume of Chile's swaps dropped from $1.9 billion in 1989 to $0.7 billion in 1990.) Swaps of public debt for private equity raise issues of inflation and government borrowing requirements that are beyond the scope of this paper.

35. Poland started its transition to the market with 8,000 or more large industrial SOEs; Czechoslovakia, Hungary, Romania, and Yugoslavia all had more than 2,500. Before its demise, the U.S.S.R., at a conservative estimate, possessed more than 47,000 very large industrial SOEs.

Bibliography

Adam, C. S. and W. P. Cavendish. 1990. "Can Privatization Succeed? Economic Structure and Programme Design in Eight Commonwealth Countries." Oxford University.

Ahmad, Muzaffer. 1990. "Privatization of Public Enterprises in Bangladesh." Paper presented at the 8th ADB/KDI Development Round Table on the Management of Public Enterprises and Privatisation, Seoul, August 22–25. Dhaka University.

Ambrose, William W., Paul R. Hennemeyer, and Jean-Paul Chapon. 1990. *Privatizing Telecommunications Systems: Business Opportunities in Developing Countries*. IFC Discussion Paper 10. Washington, D.C.: World Bank.

Asian Development Bank. 1985. *Privatization: Policies, Methods and Procedures*. Manila.

Aspe, Pedro. 1991. "Thoughts on the Structural Transformation of Mexico: The Case of Privatization of Public Sector Enterprises." Address to the Los Angeles World Affairs Council, June 21.

Berg, Elliot, and Mary Shirley. 1987. *Divestiture in Developing Countries*. World Bank Discussion Paper 11. Washington, D.C.

Bishop, Matthew, and John Kay. 1988. *Does Privatization Work? Lessons from the UK*. London: London Business School.

Bouin, O., and C. A. Michalet. 1991. *Rebalancing the Public and Private Sectors: Developing Country Experience*. Paris: Organization for Economic Cooperation and Development.

Bradburd, Ralph. 1991. "Privatization of Natural Monopoly Public Enterprises: The Regulation Issue." Policy Research Working Paper 864. World Bank, Country Economics Department, Public Sector Management and Private Sector Development Division, Washington, D.C.

Commander, Simon, and Tony Killick. 1988. "Privatisation in Developing Countries: A Survey of the Issues." In Paul Cook and Colin Kirkpatrick, eds., *Privatisation in Less Developed Countries*. New York: St. Martin's Press.

Durupty, Michel. 1991. "Privatization in France." World Bank, Country Economics Department, Public Sector Management and Private Sector Development Division, Washington, D.C.

El-Naggar, Said, ed. 1989. *Privatization and Structural Adjustment in the Arab Countries*. Washington, D.C.: International Monetary Fund.

Fukui, Koichiro. 1992. *Japanese National Railways Privatization Study: The Experience of Japan and Lessons for Developing Countries*. World Bank Discussion Paper 172. Washington, D.C.

Galal, Ahmed. 1991. *Public Enterprise Reform*. World Bank Discussion Paper 119. Washington, D.C.

———. 1990. "Does Divestiture Matter? A Framework for Learning from Experience." Policy Research Working Paper 475. World Bank, Country Economics Department, Public Sector Management and Private Sector Development Division, Washington, D.C.

Galal, Ahmed, Leroy P. Jones, Pankaj Tandon, and Ingo Vogelsang. Forthcoming. "The Welfare Consequences of Selling Public Enterprises: Case Studies from Chile, Malaysia,

Mexico, and the UK." World Bank, Country Economics Department, Public Sector Management and Private Sector Development Division, Washington, D.C.

Galenson, Alice. 1989. "Labor Redundancy in the Transport Sector: A Review." Discussion Paper 36. World Bank, Infrastructure and Urban Development Department, Washington, D.C.

Gouri, Geeta, and others. 1989. *Privatisation: The Asia-Pacific Experience.* Hyderabad, India: Institute of Public Enterprise.

Guislain, Pierre. 1992. *Divestiture of State Enterprises: An Overview of the Legal Framework.* World Bank Technical Paper 186. Washington, D.C.

Heald, David. 1990. "Privatization of Monopolies." World Bank, Country Economics Department, Public Sector Management and Private Sector Development Division, Washington, D.C.

Hegstad, Sven Olaf, and Ian Newport. 1987. *Management Contracts: Main Features and Design Issues.* World Bank Technical Paper 65. Washington, D.C.

Kikeri, Sunita. 1990. "Bank Lending for Divestiture: A Review of Experience." Policy Research Working Paper 338. World Bank, Country Economics Department, Public Sector Management and Private Sector Development Division, Washington, D.C.

Kjellstrom, Sven B. 1990. "Privatization in Turkey." Policy Research Working Paper 532. World Bank, Country Department I, Europe, Middle East, and North Africa Regional Office, Washington, D.C.

Kornai, Janos. 1990. *The Road to a Free Economy.* New York: W. W. Norton.

Lee, Barbara. 1991. "Should Employee Participation Be a Component of Privatization?" Policy Research Working Paper 664. World Bank, Country Economics Department, Public Sector Management and Private Sector Development Division, Washington, D.C.

Leeds, Roger S. 1988. *Malaysia: Genesis of a Privatization Transaction.* Cambridge, Mass.: Harvard University, Center for Business and Government.

————. 1987a. *Privatization in Jamaica: Two Case Studies.* Cambridge, Mass.: Harvard University, Center for Business and Government.

————. 1987b. *Turkey: Implementation of a Privatization Strategy.* Cambridge, Mass.: Harvard University, Center for Business and Government.

————. 1987c. *Privatization of the National Commercial Bank of Jamaica: A Case Study.* Cambridge, Mass.: Harvard University, Center for Business and Government.

Levy, Hernán, and Aurelio Menéndez. 1989. "Privatization in Transport: The Case of Port Kelang (Malaysia) Container Terminal." EDI Working Papers. World Bank, Washington, D.C.

————. 1990. "Privatization in Transport: Contracting out the Provision of Passenger Railway Services in Thailand." EDI Working Papers. World Bank, Washington, D.C.

Lorch, Klaus. 1988. *The Privatization Transaction and its Longer-Term Effects: A Case Study of the Textile Industry in Bangladesh.* Cambridge, Mass.: Harvard University, Center for Business and Government.

Luders, Rolf J. 1990. "Chile's Massive SOE Divestiture Program, 1975–1990." Paper presented at the Conference on Privatization and Ownership Changes in East and Central Europe, World Bank, Washington, D.C., June 13–14.

Marshall, Jorge, and Felipe Montt. 1987. "Privatization in Chile." Universidad de Santiago de Chile.

Megginson, William L., Robert C. Nash, and Matthias van Randenborgh. 1992. "Efficiency Gains from Privatization: An International Empirical Analysis." University of Georgia, Department of Banking and Finance, Athens.

Naqvi, Syed Nawab Haider. 1990. "The Privatization of Public Enterprises in Pakistan." Paper presented at the 8th ADB/KDI Round Table on the Management of Public Enterprises and Privatization, Seoul, August 22–25. Pakistan Institute of Development Economics, Islamabad.

Nankani, Helen. 1988. *Techniques of Privatization of State-Owned Enterprises.* Vol. 2, *Selected Country Case Studies.* World Bank Technical Paper 89. Washington, D.C.

Nellis, John. 1989a. *Contract Plans and Public Enterprise Performance.* World Bank Discussion Paper 48. Washington, D.C.

———. 1989b. "Public Enterprise Reform in Adjustment Lending." Policy Research Working Paper 233. World Bank, Country Economics Department, Public Sector Management and Private Sector Development Division, Washington, D.C.

———. 1986. *Public Enterprises in Sub-Saharan Africa.* World Bank Discussion Paper 1. Washington, D.C.

Nellis, John, and Sunita Kikeri. 1989. "Public Enterprise Reform: Privatization and the World Bank." *World Development* 17, 5 (May):659–72.

Onis, Ziya. 1991. "The Evolution of Privatization in Turkey: The Institutional Context of Public Enterprise Reform." *International Journal of Middle East Studies* 23:163–76.

Ott, Attiat F., and Keith Hartley, eds. 1991. *Privatization and Economic Efficiency: A Comparative Analysis of Developed and Developing Countries.* Brookfield, Vt.: Edward Elgar Publishers.

Perotti, Enrico C. 1991. "Transfer of Ownership and Control in Large Privatization Plans: Theory and Evidence from 10 Countries." Boston University, Boston, Mass.

Pfeffermann, Guy P., and Andrea Madarassy. 1992. *Trends in Private Investment in Developing Countries, 1992 Edition.* IFC Discussion Paper 14. Washington, D.C.: World Bank.

Poland, Ministry of Ownership Transitions. 1991. "The Dynamics of Privatization." Warsaw.

Ramanadham, V. V., ed. 1988. *Privatisation in the UK.* New York: Routledge, Chapman and Hall.

Saghir, Jamal. 1990. "Tunisian Privatization Program: Annual Report." U.S. Agency for International Development, Washington, D.C.

Sasson, Harry. 1990. "Financial Aspects of Divestiture: The Lessons of Experience in Design and Implementation." World Bank, Country Economics Department, Public Sector Management and Private Sector Development Division, Washington, D.C.

Shihata, Ibrahim F. I. 1991. *The World Bank in a Changing World.* Dordrecht, Netherlands: Nijhoff.

Shirley, Mary M. 1989a. "Improving Public Enterprise Performance: Lessons from South Korea." Policy Research Working Paper 312. World Bank, Country Economics Department, Public Sector Management and Private Sector Development Division, Washington, D.C.

———. 1989b. *The Reform of State-Owned Enterprises: Lessons from World Bank Lending.* Policy Research Report 4. Washington, D.C.

Shirley, Mary, and John Nellis. 1991. *Public Enterprise Reform: The Lessons of Experience.* EDI Development Studies. Washington, D.C.

Song, Dae Hee. 1989. *Three Essays on Korean Privatization Policy: An Overview of Privatization Policies, the People's Share Program, and a Case Study of POSCO Privatization.* Working Paper 8922. Seoul: Korea Development Institute.

Stanbury, W. T. 1988. "Privatization and the Mulroney Government, 1984–1988." In A. B. Gollner and D. Salee, eds., *Canada under Mulroney.* Montreal, Canada: Vehicule Press.

Suleiman, Ezra N. 1988. "The Politics of Privatization in Britain and France." Paper prepared for Conference on Public Sector Reform and Privatization, Center of International Studies, Princeton University, April 22–23.

Sung, Woonki. 1991. "Role of Debt Equity Swaps in Privatization." World Bank, Cofinancing Financial Advisory Services Department, Private Sector Development and Privatization Division, Washington, D.C.

Suzuki, Hiroaki. 1991. "Lessons Learned from the Guinea Privatization Program." World Bank, Africa Technical Department, Institutional Development and Management Division, Washington, D.C.

Svejnar, Jan, and Katherine Terrell. 1991. "Reducing Labor Redundancy in State-Owned Enterprises." Policy Research Working Paper 792. World Bank, Infrastructure and Urban Development Department, Transport Division, Washington, D.C.

Takano, Yoshiro. 1992. "NTT Privatization Study." World Bank, Cofinancing Financial Advisory Services Department, Private Sector Development and Privatization Division, Washington, D.C.

Taniuchi, Mitsuru. 1990. "Privatization in Japan." Paper presented at the 8th ADB/KDI Development Round Table on the Management of Public Enterprises and Privatisation, Seoul, August 22–25. Government of Japan, Economic Planning Agency, Tokyo.

Togo, Ministry of Industry. 1989. "Privatisation, Restructuration, Liquidation d'Enterprises Publiques: Propositions de Stratégie pour la Poursuite de l'Action d'Allegement du Secteur Parapublic." Lomé.

Triche, Thelma A. 1990. "Private Participation in the Delivery of Water Supply Services: The Case of Guinea." World Bank, Infrastructure and Urban Development Department, Water and Sanitation Division, Washington, D.C.

United Nations. 1989. *Role and Extent of Competition in Improving the Performance of Public Enterprises.* Proceedings of a UN Interregional Seminar on Performance Improvement of Public Enterprises, New Delhi, April 12–19. New York.

United Nations Development Programme. 1989. *A Study of the Experience with Privatization of Public Enterprises in Developing Countries.* New York.

Veljanovski, Cento. 1989. *Privatisation and Competition: A Market Prospectus.* London: Institute of Economic Affairs.

————. 1987. *Selling the State: Privatization in Britain.* London: Weidenfeld and Nicolson.

Vickers, John, and George Yarrow. 1988. *Privatization: An Economic Analysis.* Cambridge, Mass.: MIT Press.

Vuylsteke, Charles. 1988. *Techniques of Privatization of State-Owned Enterprises.* Vol. 1, *Methods and Implementation.* World Bank Technical Paper 88. Washington, D.C.

Wellenius, Björn, Peter A. Stern, Timothy E. Nulty, and Richard D. Stern. 1989. *Restructuring and Managing the Telecommunications Sector.* A World Bank Symposium. Washington, D.C.

World Bank. 1991a. "Developing the Private Sector: The World Bank's Experience and Approach." Country Economics Department, Public Sector Management and Private Sector Development Division, Washington, D.C.

————. 1991b. "The Evolution, Situation, and Prospects of the Electric Power Sector in the Latin American and Caribbean Countries." Report 7. World Bank, Latin America and the Caribbean Regional Office, Infrastructure and Energy Division, Washington, D.C.

————. 1991c. *The Reform of Public Sector Management: The Lessons of Experience.* County Economics Department. Policy Research Report 18. Washington, D.C.

————. 1983. *World Development Report 1983.* New York: Oxford University Press.

Xiao, Geng. 1991. "Managerial Autonomy, Fringe Benefits, and Ownership Structure: A Comparative Study of Chinese State and Collective Enterprises." *China Economic Review* 2 (1): 47–73.